Living in a Foreign Language

Also by Michael Tucker
I Never Forget a Meal: An Indulgent Reminiscence

Living in a Foreign Language

A Memoir of Food, Wine, and Love in Italy

Michael Tucker

Photographs by Kristine Walsh

Atlantic Monthly Press
New York

Published simultaneously in Canada
Printed in the United States of America

FIRST EDITION

Library of Congress Cataloging-in-Publication Data

Tucker, Michael, 1944–
    Living in a foreign language: a memoir of food, wine, and love in Italy / Michael Tucker.
        p.   cm.
    ISBN-10: 0-87113-962-6
    ISBN-13: 978-0-87113-962-7
    1. Spoleto Region (Italy)—Description and travel.   2. Spoleto Region (Italy)—Social life and customs.   3. Tucker, Michael, 1944–   4. Cookery, Italian.   5. Wine and wine making—Italy.   I. Title.

DG975.S75T83   2007
945'.651—dc22   2006052626

Atlantic Monthly Press
an imprint of Grove/Atlantic, Inc.
841 Broadway
New York, NY 10003

Distributed by Publishers Group West
www.groveatlantic.com

07   08   09   10   11   12   10   9   8   7   6   5   4   3   2   1

Sempre Jill

Umbria

"Avrai tu L'universo, resti L'Italia a me."
You may have the universe, if I may have Italy.
—Giuseppe Verdi

"We can be bought, but we cannot be bored."
*Possiamo essere comprati, ma non possiamo
essere annoiati.*
—Alfred Lunt & Lynn Fontanne

Living in a Foreign Language

One

THERE'S A HILL COVERED WITH OLIVE TREES that nestles around our house like the strong, safe lap of an infinitely patient grandfather. We called it a mountain until we hiked up to the top one day and saw the snowcapped Sibillini stretching out across the horizon. No, it's a hill—one of many *colline* that climb to the east of us and roll out to the north and south, shimmering with silver-green olive leaves as far as you can see. The tiny stone house sits tucked into the side of the hill so that our bedroom window isn't exposed to the early rays of the sun, but that morning I was up with the first soft light in the sky. I had slept the sleep of the sated. Perhaps the three glasses of grappa at the end of dinner had helped a bit with that. Along with the bottomless pitcher of the local red wine that went down so easily with the wood-grilled lamb and the fried potatoes. God, those potatoes. Maybe it was all a dream; I never eat potatoes after a big bowl of pasta. Not in the same meal. Not in real life. The pasta, by the way, had been simple—just noodles in olive oil with about a half-pound of fresh truffles shaved over the top. Truffles pop out of the ground like weeds around here.

The sky did a cross-fade from gray to light blue and one by one the birds started to sing. I had nowhere to go for a couple of hours; I just lay there and listened to them. I had flown over two days earlier to close the deal on this farmhouse in the hills of Umbria and I was heading back to California later that afternoon. My inner clock was totally confused at this point, but sleep wasn't really the issue; I could sleep some other time.

The Rustico—that's its name—has been standing on this hill looking west out onto the vast and verdant Spoleto valley for over 350 years. "Rustico" means a farm workers' cottage, a place where migrant workers slept when they came every year to harvest the olives. Now it was going to shelter two migrant actors.

I went down to the kitchen and made a pot of coffee. I sat at the table under the pergola just outside the kitchen door and watched a bird with black and white striped plumage and a smart-ass Woody Woodpecker look on his face squawk and swoop down from the trees, strafe the vegetable garden and then soar up for a couple of laps around the chimney. You could already tell it was going to be a hot day. But inside the Rustico, with its three-foot- thick stone walls—which make it look considerably larger on the outside than it feels inside—it was as cool as a wine cellar.

I called Jill in California, where it was nine o'clock the evening before. Totally confusing. I told her all about yesterday's meeting at the *notaio*'s office, where I signed the papers and passed over the certified checks—one above the table, one below. I told her how the *notaio* solemnly intoned the whole contract, pausing after every line for the English

The Rustico

translation. It all felt quite official. I told her how Bruno and Mayes, who sold us the house, and JoJo, who brokered the deal, took me out to lunch afterward at Fontanelle, a restaurant a few miles up the hill from our new house.

I told Jill how I was feeling at that moment, sitting next to the garden watching the birds; about the pull this place has for me, how the rhythm of the land dictates the pace for everything and everyone. I'm not a particularly patient person—I don't usually do the stillness thing well—but I thought that living in this house, in this valley, might change that some.

The year we met—1969 at the Arena Stage in Washington, D.C.—I was already married with a one-year-old little girl, and Jill was engaged to an actor who was working up in Montreal. We caught each other's eye in the read-through of that season's opening play and by the time we got to dress rehearsal, we were waist-deep in a love affair that's lasted for thirty-five years and counting. A few days after the closing play of the season, I left my marriage, and a month after that Jill and I took custody of Alison, my daughter. Then we left for New York to try our luck on Broadway, off-Broadway and—mostly—the unemployment office. That was the first time we stepped off the edge together, and it's become a way of life with us.

We have nine-year cycles. At least, looking back, that seems to be the way it works out. New York, however, was a doubleheader—almost eighteen years in the trenches, carving out our careers, learning to live with long periods of separation and falling prey to the pitfalls and temptations of life on location. Alison grew up there. I took her to school—every day on the back of my bicycle, rain or shine—and when we left, she stayed on in the apartment and went to college there. Max, our son, was born in Lenox Hill Hospital and went—every day on the back of my bicycle—to the Montessori School on West 99th Street. New York was our nest. We met our dearest friends there, the kind of friends that even if we don't see them for ten years are still our dearest friends. Our personalities took shape there—individually, as a family and as a couple.

Then in 1986, we got a call from Steven Bochco, an old friend of mine from all the way back to college days, with an offer to do his new TV series. He had written the roles for us, he said. Jill got on the phone, thanked him graciously but told him that she was really a theater actress and didn't want to leave New York. Her kids were in good schools; she was a nester; she didn't want to be on TV. I was across the room screaming at her to sell out—sell out at any price!

But I needn't have worried. Bochco calmed her and said

she didn't have to play the part, but was it okay with her if he kept her in mind—just to help him write it? She—again graciously—deigned to allow him to do this.

When the script showed up, Jill started to leaf through it and, after a few pages, started learning the lines. No way was she going to let anyone else play that part.

We flew out to L.A. for three weeks in May to shoot the pilot. It was a high time—first-class parts in a first-class pilot, custom-made clothes, studio flacks and agents hovering around us; it was like a scene in a movie. And we were doing it together. After years of one of us being up while the other was out of work, here we were taking our first stroll down the sidewalk of fame together, arm in arm, both winners, no loser.

We came back to New York after we shot the pilot to get our kids together, our things together, so that we could move out to L.A. in August to shoot the rest of the first season. We went to St. Martin in the Caribbean to celebrate and on the day we got back to New York, Jill reached up and felt a lump in her breast.

It was cancer. We lay down on our bed on West Eighty-ninth Street, pulled the shades and held hands in the dark. Jill was looking at the end of her life. I was looking at life without her. Like a drowning man, I watched all the scenes of our life together and realized how much of my identity had been tied up with this exquisite woman. Just standing next to her elevated what other people thought of me, what I thought of myself. I had cashed a lot of checks on that account. Not a pretty thought, but there it was.

Jill had her operation at Mt. Sinai in New York. Two weeks later she would have her first radiation appointment at UCLA—on the very same day *L.A. Law* went into production.

We packed up, calmed our terrified children and got on the plane for L.A. This time we weren't only changing coasts, jobs, schools, lifestyles and friends; we were also taking on a new life partner: cancer. This partner would radically change the way we looked at ourselves, our relationship, our future together—everything. Eventually—once we accepted it— cancer taught us how to live.

The sun appeared over the top of the mountain a little after eight and I got in the car and went down to our little village. I had an espresso at the bar; then I had another. I was too shy to start a conversation with the barista, so I pretended to read a local newspaper in which every fifth or sixth word made sense. After the morning crowd thinned out a bit I summoned up the courage to talk. I opened with my well-practiced phrase of self-abasement: *"I'm so sorry, I'm an American, I don't speak very well in Italian. . . ."* This always worked. The barman lit up and we had a third-grade-level conversation in Italian in which I asked him if he could tell me where to buy the best local olive oil. He launched into a vivid description, with maps drawn on paper napkins, of where he thought I should go.

I wanted to take as much of Umbria back with me to California as I could fit into my suitcase. I found the olive oil outlet, where they also had some chestnut honey the region is known for and some cellophane bags of *strangozzi,* the local pasta. Then I stopped at a house—right on our road— that had a sign out front advertising fresh truffles. It turned out to be quite a serious operation—aluminum bins of truffles with the earth still clinging to them, scales to calculate their worth down to the smallest gram and a shrink-wrap machine so that people like me could travel without creating too much of a stink. I bought six beautiful specimens, each about the size of a billiard ball, to smuggle through customs. I went to the wine store to pick up six bottles of Montefalco Rosso. It's a wonderful wine, which I hoped would taste as good when I got it back to California.

I went back to the house with my booty and stuffed it all into the suitcase, among the few clothes I had with me. I locked up, closed the shutters and drove off to the airport in Rome, bidding *arrivederci* to our little Rustico until we'd be back in September.

Two

We had two events scheduled within a day of each other that
summed up the chaos that was our last year in Los Angeles.
Friday night was a party held for a few thousand network affiliates that NBC hosted every year, and the night before was
a small gathering at a friend's house—she's a TV producer
and budding New Ager who'd just shared with us that she
was channeling Jesus Christ on a regular basis. The idea was
that we would go to her place for a little dinner, and then
afterward—in the media room—we'd have a séance with
the Son of God.

"Bring questions!" she'd reminded us.

Well, yeah.

The Friday night party turned out to be a religious experience in its own right. It's the event that NBC annually lav-
ishes on its station managers from all over the country—a
week of boozing and schmoozing and informational meetings

where NBC gets the chance to trot out its plans for the new season. The party is a peak event where all the network stars come out to play and rub shoulders for a couple of hours with the "flyover people"—a charming Hollywood term for everyone who doesn't live in New York or L.A.

We'd been doing this gig for eight years and had the drill down pat. Our limo pulled up to the Beverly Hilton at six-thirty—a little early to be stylishly late but not bad. We were glowing, like the stars we had become—tanned, coifed, ready to shoot the gauntlet of photographers, reporters, *Entertainment Tonight* and E! network interviewers, tossing off bon mots as we moved briskly toward the bar.

"Ah, Mike and Jill, the wittiest couple in Hollywood" they'd all probably say.

But as we disembarked our limo, there were no photographers to snap us, no gauntlet to run and no reporters shouting our names. A small drop of sweat trickled down the inside of my Valentino shirt. Could it be the wrong night? Or the wrong hotel? Was it the Beverly Wilshire? Or worse, the Sheraton Universal, all the way over on the other side of the hill?

The lobby was empty, too. Of celebrities, that is. There were other people—regular people—but you can't imagine how easy it is to tell the difference. I looked back at the curb but the limo had already pulled away—to go to that place where limos go when they, too, are empty of celebrities. Then we saw a face we recognized—a girl from the network publicity department whom we'd worked with many times.

"Why are you guys here?" she asked with genuine alarm. "The party starts at eight! The affiliates are all in a meeting in the other ballroom that doesn't break for at least another hour."

Eight? Oh, Christ. There was little hope we could be

stylishly late unless we somehow found our limo and went back home for a while. We stood there in the lobby and tried to pinpoint the blame for this debacle. Was it her department or our publicist who'd gotten it wrong? Probably our guy—he'd been phoning it in ever since we turned down the cover for the *Good Housekeeping* sweater issue.

Blame aside, we didn't want to go back to the house. Once you've got your look together, it's depressing to watch your kids eat Chinese takeout. It takes the glow away.

"You know, we've got a little pressroom—God knows it's not very fancy, but that's where we're all hanging out until the party starts. At least you can relax for a while, have a glass of wine."

Wine. Okay. I was trying to maintain a balance between the huffy, put-out star and the down-to-earth good guy that I had become famous for, but it wasn't easy. She led us off to a room that had been set up with tables and chairs, phones and a few TV monitors that carried the meeting from the other ballroom on closed circuit. We sat at our own little table, and all the other people in the room—PR folk, network flunkies, reporters waiting for a tidbit, photographers cooling their heels until the big stars arrived—made a space around us as if we were an alien species.

I downed my wine and started on Jill's. I wasn't feeling comfortable in this room. These were the very same people who would have been fawning over us—calling out our names, begging us to pose for photos, reminding us how wonderful and unique we were—if we had just come an hour later and made a proper star's entrance. Now, they were eyeing us from across the room like we were bad meat.

I started stewing. Our publicist had done this on purpose. He was tired of trying to pump life into our fading careers so he decided to humiliate us in front of the press. To stab us in the back. I mean it's hard enough being a star, but when there's nobody there to worship you, it's damn near impossible.

And then it occurred to me that this was a situation that would have been fully appreciated by Jesus, whom—via our friend's channeling—we'd had dinner with the night before. He knew the drill. He'd felt the adulation and then had it taken away. He'd felt the betrayal. I sat there nursing my wounds, identifying with Jesus Christ—and I won't deny it made me feel a lot better.

Jesus, by the way, had been totally delightful. This wasn't the Jesus stuck up there on the cross with that "I died for your sins" look in his eye. This was the young visionary Jesus: charming, soft-spoken, quite funny—not Henny Youngman or anything, but with a nice sense of irony, gave you the feeling that he understood the way of the world. I thought about telling him the one about Moses and Jesus playing golf. I should have; he would have enjoyed it. Bottom line I really liked him. Actually a lot more than our friend who was channeling him. She should maybe think about being him on a more permanent basis.

We'd arrived at her house with high expectations. Not that we thought we were actually going to meet Christ—we weren't that far gone—but curious as to how she would try to pull this off. During dinner, she gave us the setup, about how she was as amazed by the phenomenon as we were, that she didn't understand how it worked—the standard channeling crap.

But when we got into the session, she got herself out of the way pretty quickly—no theatrics, no fanfare, she just closed her eyes and we all waited a bit. Jill later told me that at this point she felt an energy shift in the room and that it gave her goose bumps. But remember, this is Jill we're talking about—the goose bump queen. The only thing I could feel was anxiety as to whether this was going to be embarrassing. If Jill is good at sensing energy, I take the prize in being able to pick up flop sweat.

After a long while, she started to speak—or rather, he started to speak, because it was definitely not her voice.

"Perhaps the best way to start would be for you to ask me something," said Jesus. He had an accent. Aramaic, I would say—although I wouldn't know an Aramanian if I tripped over one. But it sounded a little Aramaic to me.

"How're you doing?" That was all I could think of to ask.

"Very well, thank you."

"We'd like to thank you for . . . being with us tonight" said Jill, always courteous.

"It is a pleasure."

Like I said, he was a very nice guy—easy to talk to, totally nonthreatening.

"Do you come here often?" That was me—a totally stupid thing to say. I was just trying to get the ball rolling, but I realized it came off like I was trying to pick him up at a bar. Everybody—including Jesus—kind of looked away and pretended I hadn't said it.

"Ask what is in your heart," he said after a pause.

"Can you tell us where we'll be next year?" asked Jill. "I mean, will we stay here or move to a new place?"

He smiled at both of us—a beautiful smile that made us feel approved of.

"Your journey has already begun."

This was the perfect thing to say. Jill was beaming. How could he know us so well? I was a little less impressed. I mean our friend who was channeling him knew very well that we were already on a journey. We had talked to her many times about all the New Age stuff we'd been doing—meditation, tantra, Chinese herbs. So it wouldn't have been difficult for her to pass this information on to him—or Him, I guess I should say. She wouldn't even have to tell Him because she *was* Him for the moment—or He was her—or whatever.

"You will move to a house with a circle of pines outside your bedroom window."

Now this was a little better—an actual prediction, something we could document.

"Sounds wonderful," said Jill, still beaming.

This chitchat went on for a while. Whenever we tried to pin him down to specifics, he reminded us that "Life has its own plan" or "Your path will present itself in unexpected ways." I don't recall any other flat-on predictions like the circle of pines, but in general, he seemed to think we were headed in the right direction. Our journey had already begun and that, according to Jesus, was a good thing.

Exactly how far along we were on this journey didn't reveal itself until the following evening in the makeshift pressroom at the Beverly Hilton Hotel. There was a TV monitor on the table next to us carrying the affiliates' meeting from the ballroom down the hall. And as I sat there, sopping up second-rate wine, brooding on the vicissitudes of fame, snarling at the perfidy of our publicist, I became aware of Don Ohlmeyer speaking on the TV about the coming season—about how NBC was going to deliver a whopping audience to all the local eleven o'clock news shows every night. Ohlmeyer had recently moved over from the sports department and had been made head of NBC West Coast or some such thing. NBC had more heads than it knew how to feed.

". . . And the most important announcement of the

evening is that we're going to finally retire that old war-horse, *L.A. Law,* and put her out to pasture where she belongs. We have a new show in the works that will make ten o'clock on Thursday nights the most watched hour in television."

I don't think I actually heard it when he said it—they say you never hear the one that gets you. Jill and I flicked a look to each other and then quickly flicked away—as if we instantaneously agreed to deny what we'd just heard. Then, as he droned on with the particulars, the reality dripped into my body—like an IV with a lethal injection.

Drip. The bitterest truth of all—he was right. The show *was* old and tired. We had played out all the stories and then gone back around and played them again. Time to put it out of its misery.

Drip. Rejection—right into the heart. It wasn't just the show they were tired of—it was us. They'd seen our shtick; it worked for a while, now it was time for someone new.

Drip. The money. Oh my God, the money. We were about to take the biggest salary cut in the history of the world. My world, at least. Did I save enough? Can you ever save enough?

Drip. The money again. Did I play it wrong? Did I try to cash in on our fame so much that people developed contempt for us? Yeah, I did. They did.

Drip. Drip. Dead.

So, what now? We could hold on like hell; I know people who have parlayed their diminishing fame into years of celebrity—decades. Just by traveling to smaller and smaller cities. You may not be able to get a seat at Spago but they'll throw a fucking parade for you in Pittsburgh.

Or we could return to the relative purity of our life in the theater. Recycled TV stars were all the rage in New York.

I looked at Jill again—really looked this time. Her eyes were blue and deep. They were more worried for me than for her. She didn't care all that much about money and fame—she never had. She slipped me a smile that said, "Don't worry, we'll be all right." But I didn't feel all right. Anger was bubbling up—my typical response to fear.

"Who is this *Wide World of Sports* hack talking about us like we're an old bag of shit?" I wanted to say. "We carried NBC for eight years—we *invented* Thursday night at ten o'clock."

But I didn't say anything. Instead, I recalled the lesson that Jesus had taught us the night before—that our path would reveal itself in unexpected ways. Yeah, but *this* unexpected? Don Ohlmeyer as the angel of destiny? It's enough to shake your faith.

Jill and I walked out of the hotel, arm in arm, into the warm May evening. We weren't TV stars anymore, just people. It would take some getting used to, but we could do it. We'd have fun with it. Maybe we'd find a seminar—a week at Esalen—"Re-Humbling," or "Embracing Your Obscurity." Hell, we started out as real people; it wouldn't be so hard to get back to it.

"Oh my God!" A woman who was checking in to the hotel with her family recognized us.

"Can you wait here one second? I'll be right back!"

She herded her husband and three small children over to where we were standing. She knelt by her children and admonished them sternly.

"You look very carefully at these two people, you hear me?"

She pointed to us like we were a stop sign.

"They are on TV. And one day when you're older you'll

see them on reruns and know who they are. These are real live stars."

She didn't know we were already on reruns.

"Now, give each one an autograph. I want you to sign, 'You met me at the Beverly Hilton Hotel.' Then sign one for Elizabeth, one for Peter James and one for little Jessica. Do you have a pen?"

I told her I didn't and she looked at me with contempt. I borrowed a pen and paper from the doorman and we signed the autographs. Then she had her husband take pictures of us with all of the children and then with each one separately. She thought she owned us.

While they were snapping away I felt Jill squeeze my hand, which meant, "Let's get out of here." I looked over my shoulder and saw an empty taxi with its door hanging open. Thank you, Jesus! We jumped in and snuggled down into the cracked leather seats like two kids playing hide-and-seek. We held hands and I felt a sudden rush of relief mixed with euphoria mixed with an optimism I'd never felt before—I knew I could get through anything as long as I could hold her hand. After a while the driver turned around.

"Where ya headed?"

Damned if we knew. The only thing clear to me—crystal clear—was that if I had a choice between spending an evening with Jesus Christ or with Don Ohlmeyer, I wouldn't have to think for a second.

We opened our windows to get rid of the old-taxi smell and gave him our address. It was no limo, but it would get us home.

Three

WE FOUND OUR CIRCLE OF PINES—right outside the bedroom window of a rambling old house in Marin County, Northern California. We found a great school for our son, Max, and we got to know a whole new group of friends. The Bay Area is a food lover's paradise, so we gave up nothing on that score. We would go back to L.A. for the occasional TV movie or guest shot; or do a play maybe once a year in San Francisco or Marin; but mostly we focused on things other than career. It was the first time since we'd been together that a job—or the promise of a job—didn't dictate where and how we lived, which was liberating and frightening at the same time. While we were trying to figure out what was next, Jill reminded me that our life had always worked best when the two of us were good together, solidly in love. We knew if we could get that part right everything else would fall into place just fine. So we decided to use our newfound freedom and time to explore . . . well, each other.

We took courses. Marin County is the world center of

self-improvement so we had no trouble finding courses, seminars and weekend retreats in which to delve into the more arcane aspects of the "man/woman paradigm." We took lots of courses in communication; we attended lectures by various experts who talked about what men want as opposed to what women want. And we took courses on sex. On sex, about sex and all around sex. And I must say it came as a surprise to me how much there was to learn on that subject.

This was all going along wonderfully until one afternoon, at the checkout counter of the Mill Valley Market, the cashier asked me to sign something. I looked down and it was the front page of some tabloid with the headline, "*L.A. Law* Stars in Kinky Sex Cult." Which was, by the way, incorrect in all aspects—in that we hadn't been stars for a while, our sex life had no noticeable kinks and the only group we had joined in all the years of our marriage was the Automobile Club of Northern California.

It seems, though, that we had talked too much. We had come off like missionaries, bringing the couples of the world to a higher plane—you can imagine how boring we were. We lost some friends. The jobs dwindled. We became fringe people, which was okay except when we saw someone we knew in a movie or on TV playing a role that we'd have been good in. That still irked.

Money became an issue. We were still living the lifestyle of the rich and famous, without earning any income to speak of. The pressure of our dwindling bank balance started to undermine our little paradise. So I decided to get an appraisal on our house in Big Sur. This was our getaway place, our dream house, perched on a ridge between the mountains and the sea that we built when the TV money was flowing like water. I had to approach Jill carefully about this idea, because she had often said in moments of great tenderness that we would grow old together in that house. I was concerned that we would just grow poor. It wasn't that Big Sur cost us that much out of pocket—we had built it for cash—but after the appraisal it was clear that it was worth too much for us not to sell it.

"Home" is a funny word; it means different things to different people. Jill grew up an only child; her dad's business required the family to move every year, so she was perennially the new kid in school. She grew up to become a nester with a vengeance—ostensibly for her kids, but for her own peace of mind as well. For Jill, home is a cause.

I, on the other hand, couldn't wait to get away from my roots—nice people and all, but I was more interested in seeing the world, checking out how the gentiles lived. And whereas Jill and I had had a series of homes over the last thirty years, I'd never thought twice about selling one in order to move on to the next. For me, home was a base for the next adventure. This was always an area of tension between us, and when I sold the Big Sur house, thinking to put us in good financial shape, I broke her heart.

Then when Max, our youngest, got ready to leave for college, our different philosophies of mothering and fathering came into conflict as well. Jill was feeling extremely umbilical about the whole thing. Not that I was blasé, mind you—I would miss Max enormously. But I thought of his going off to college more as a celebration. He had gotten into his first-choice school, he was pursuing his dream of a career in music, he felt confident in himself, he was sure of his path. As a dad, I felt, frankly, successful—not an emotion I'd experienced in this area all that often. But for Jill, his departure was a wrenching loss, the fatal final curtain on a role she'd been playing with total commitment and steely determination for thirty-three years. So, while I was chilling the bottle of champagne to celebrate our incipient liberation, Jill was quietly gearing up to play the last act of *Medea*.

So I blundered right in—while she was reeling from the loss of her home and her baby—to convince her that what we really needed to do was buy a house in Italy. This was an old bone of contention between us. I had tried for years, in vain, to convince her that we should buy a house in the south of France—in Ramatuelle, just outside Saint Tropez. There's a beach there five miles long filled with young, naked women. I couldn't understand why she wasn't interested.

Then, a couple of years later, a friend asked me why I wanted to buy a house in the south of France and I told him it was because it was so close to Italy. Eureka! Ever since then I'd been trying to sell Jill on the idea of a house in Italy. And now that Max had left for college in New York, I pushed even harder.

Jill was understandably cool. She couldn't get why, if we'd had to get rid of her dream house in Big Sur, we would plunge into buying another house—especially one that was six thousand miles away. For me it made perfect sense: The Italian house wouldn't cost us a fraction of what we earned from the sale of Big Sur; our nest was empty and forlorn; we had—regrettably or not—no professional reason to hang around; and we were at a perfect time in our life to start a new cycle—to learn a new language in an exquisite, ancient country, to meet new friends. Now was our time to travel—while we could still do stairs. Now was our time to savor the glories of Italian cuisine—while we still had our original teeth. Now was the time to take a romantic plunge together—while our plumbing was still up and functioning. Jill looked at me like I was crazy. Or worse, she told me that if I really wanted it, it was okay with her. This is the kiss of death. If I learned one thing from all those courses we took, when she says, "If you really want it, it's okay with me," she's actually saying, "I don't want this." And who needs to be in Italy with a woman who doesn't want to be there— who's unhappy with me for insisting on my own agenda? Not going to work. What I could do was occasionally put it in front of her—like an item on a menu that she might one day develop a taste for—and wait to see if she bit.

So, a year later, when a friend of ours, Birgit, invited us to her sixtieth birthday party, I saw my shot. Birgit was born in Germany, lives in Mill Valley and is building a house in Tahoe with her husband, but her birthday party was to be in Puglia, at the very southern tip of the heel of Italy. Which tells you something about Birgit.

I used the occasion to propose a trip that would take us the entire length of the Italian Peninsula. After making a solemn promise that I wouldn't buy a house, we flew off for a month's journey that would give us a taste of Italy, from stem to stern.

Third in our party—and party it was—was our friend Caroline, who had also been invited to Birgit's birthday. We first met Caroline when she'd worked for us as a personal assistant—a job, by the way, that you shouldn't give to a dog. If I had to be my personal assistant I'd shoot myself. But Caroline thrived—perhaps because she'd spent her first four years as an orphan in South Korea and after that even our job looked good. Over the years, the three of us became such good friends—living in the same house, traveling together, manning the calendar together, raising our dogs together—that we finally had to fire her. So now she's part of the family. She travels well, having grown up with her adopted parents in India, Pakistan and Indonesia before moving to Europe for what she calls her "professional years." She speaks five languages fluently—English, perhaps, not quite as fluently.

Caroline and Jill have grown together over the years— as confidantes, fierce supporters of each other, sisters in the great fight, as it were—and have formed a unit in our house that stands as a powerful counterbalance to the rampant male ego that is me. Whereas I can usually bully my way past one of them, or do an end-around sneak past the other, the two of them back each other up—not unlike a pair of all-pro defensive backs—in such a way as to make male dominance in my household more and more difficult to maintain. Not impossible, mind you, just more difficult.

Caroline tends to be brutally honest. I think it's a Korean thing. This trait generally makes me want to sneak out the back door when I see her coming; but Jill seems to value Caroline's brand of tough love more and more as the years go by. Last year, when Jill and I were doing a play together, Caroline came to see a final dress rehearsal and afterward we casually asked her what she thought. Not being of the theater, she had no idea as to the protocol in dealing with the sensitive egos of actors about to open a play, and she blurted out to Jill that she thought she should be "bigger, more theatrical, go all the way with it." I sat there holding my breath, not believing that Caroline would dare trample into Jill's private domain, her art. I know I certainly wouldn't. But Jill just sat there, nodding for a minute, thanked her and then went into the office for a couple of hours to work. The next night, her performance took on a whole new size and dimension—nothing, mind you, that hadn't been there before, but with a hell of a lot more assurance. No way would she have taken that criticism from me.

Jill won't buy a dress or shoes without running it by Caroline first. Caroline won't take a step toward a new boyfriend without first having extensive coaching sessions with Jill. It's a very complicated relationship. They serve as mirrors for each other, support systems, truth-tellers. And they torment each other on a fairly daily basis as well. Caroline is envious of Jill's beauty, her stature, her success—both in career and in relationship; Jill is envious of Caroline's youth, her athleticism, her ability to turn heads as she walks down the street, her parade of admiring male suitors.

Off to Italy

For me? Well, all I can say is that life has never been so interesting. Not a cakewalk, mind you, but very, very interesting. If men are from Mars and women from Venus, I guess what happened in our household is that Venus now has a lot more clout than she did before. She holds her opinion in a much clearer, more assertive way. Which—when I can get past the ego part—actually makes my life much easier. Because all I want to do is to give Jill everything she wants, and now I have a much clearer idea of what that is.

So we were three for the road, taking a month to drive from the Alps to the very southernmost tip of Puglia. Because I was the head planner, our itinerary skirted churches, castles, museums and such, and focused in a very direct way on food and wine. Of course, if we saw a church that piqued our interest—great. If a museum called out to us to see its paintings—by all means. But the overriding mandate was to eat well and to be in places intrinsically Italian—mostly in smaller towns, usually overlooking something beautiful: the sea, or a hillside of grape vines or olive trees. Our goal was to slow down our hearts and minds until they synched up with the circadian rhythm of the Italian countryside.

First we drove to Alba in the Piemonte, the home of my favorite wines, of Slow Food and white truffles—one of the gastronomic treasure troves of Italy. We booked into a little bed-and-breakfast just outside of town. The owner, Roberta, is a foodie and knows all the inside spots where the best local cooking is being turned out. After long breakfasts of fresh yogurt and Roberta's just-picked berries, we spent our days driving up and down the vine-covered hills between little villages named Barbaresco, Barolo and Neive.

Then we were off to the Cinque Terre—for fresh grilled anchovies, pristine white wine that grows on the vertical hillsides overlooking the sea and pasta *al pesto* in the very place it had been born. If there is a more beautiful town than Vernazza, I have not seen it. Every day Caroline, who is a triathlete in her spare time, led us on backbreaking hikes up and down the vineyards to burn off at least some of the calories we were picking up at lunch.

Our plan was to stay at a bed-and-breakfast in Tuscany for a few days, then head down to Sorrento, where we'd also get a chance to see (and taste) the pleasures of Naples. Then it would be on to Puglia for a week of birthday partying and, finally, Rome, where we would spend a few days before catching our flight home.

Serendipitously, we planned a little afternoon side trip from our B and B in Tuscany to Spoleto, in Umbria, where a friend of a friend had told us about a restaurant experience, a farmhouse on the top of a mountain, that sounded too good to be missed.

That's where fate interceded. The place in Tuscany was not what we had hoped for. It seemed the proprietors were the foremost collectors of Art Deco in the entire Tuscan countryside. So, zebra-striped chaises stood beside lip-shaped coffee tables next to Bauhaus desks with satin-covered side chairs. It was a nightmare. The bedrooms were gloomy and damp and, after a really depressing breakfast of cold toast and instant coffee, we had a little meeting over in the corner of the yard.

"Honey, we don't want to stay here anymore."

Caroline nodded solemnly in agreement.

"Yeah, but I've already paid for three nights. And it wasn't cheap."

The two girls stared at me. They didn't have to say a word.

"Where will we go?"

"Anywhere else," said Jill. "We could go to Sorrento a little earlier."

"Or maybe Positano," offered Caroline. We had been there for just a day a few years before and had loved it.

"I'm kind of fixated on that farmhouse lunch that we've booked for tomorrow—over in Spoleto," I said. "Why don't we try to find a place there."

So I called a woman named Joanna Ross who had been recommended to me by the same friend who'd given us the lunch tip. Joanna is an American who had relocated with her husband and son to Spoleto some ten years before. Before that she was a William Morris agent in New York. It turns out that she had been one of our agents for a time but because she was in New York and we were in L.A., we'd never actually met.

"Joanna? Hi. I'm Michael Tucker and, uh, we're the people who are doing that lunch tomorrow at the farmhouse? I think you helped set that up?"

"Yeah, at Patrico."

"Well, we hate where we're staying in Tuscany," I told her. "Can we find anything nice—you know, not fancy, just beautiful, local, charming—over in your area?"

"I'll call you back in ten minutes."

She took my cell phone number and hung up. I felt not unlike the way I feel when I talk to my agent in Los Angeles—like I'm not the most important thing on his mind right at that moment. But less than ten minutes later, she called back with exactly what I had asked for.

"Okay. There's a hotel called Il Castello di Poreta. It's a castle from the fourteenth century. I know the people who renovated it and opened it up as a B and B. It's owned by the *comune,* the local town, but my friends have a long lease on it. They'll give you a great deal—the inside price. You'll love it."

She generously offered to meet us just outside Spoleto and lead us on to the Castello. We swapped cell phone numbers and made a plan to meet in a couple of hours. The three of us checked out of our Tuscany place with a story about how our plans had changed. The owners put on long faces and explained, artfully and decorously, that they couldn't give any of our money back and we packed the car and crossed over the border into Umbria and our destiny.

Four

WE MET JOANNA IN THE PARKING LOT of the Volks-
wagen dealership in the industrial section of Spoleto. We
had been waiting a good half hour and were getting worried
that we had the wrong place when, finally, she pulled into
the driveway.

"Hi, kids. Been waiting long?"

We nodded.

"Well, that's Italy. Get used to it."

Her accent was hard to place. There was definitely a bit
of British—she had been born in England and both her parents are Brits—mixed with a dialect that can only be described as "New York theatrical agent–speak," a patois
developed from years of bullying, coddling, negotiating and
demanding for fourteen hours a day over the telephone.

"Hop in your car. I'll lead you to the Castello."

On the way, we passed below the Ponte delle Torre, the
splendid ancient aqueduct connecting Spoleto to Monteluco,
and followed Joanna's little Fiat north on the Via Flaminia a
few miles to Poreta. This highway that connects all the towns

and villages in that part of Umbria is the very same Via
Flaminia that the Romans built in the third century B.C. to
connect Rome to Rimini. Now—with gas stations, outdoor
furniture stores, lumber yards and nurseries—it looks a bit
more like the Miracle Mile on the outskirts of Pittsburgh.
After a mile or two, Joanna pulled over onto a little side road
and we parked behind her and got out.

"You see that town up there?"

She gestured over the valley toward a mountain north of
us. On it was a pristine, white, walled city dominating that
part of the valley.

"That's Campello Alto. Then over here"—she pointed
south to another hilltop—"is the Castello. That's where
you'll be staying. Back in the Middle Ages, these two towns
would declare war on each other every couple of years.
Whenever they got bored."

We drove up the steep road to the Castello, emptied our
luggage out of the car and entered through a huge portal that
stood in the half-ruined wall of the castle. The view of the
valley stopped us dead in our tracks. To the south is Spoleto
itself; to the north, Campello Alto, Trevi and beyond, Spello,
Foligno and Assisi. Across the valley, there's Montefalco, the
wine center of central Umbria, and beyond the hills, Todi.
These medieval (and older) hill towns dominate the valley
and look down on a broad expanse of tobacco farms, vineyards and endless miles of olive trees. I flashed on that moment in *Lost Horizon* when the pilgrims rounded the mountain
pass and first gazed down on Shangri-la. This was a definite
upgrade from the Art Deco museum in Tuscany.

We checked in and met Luca, the manager of the hotel,
who showed us to our rooms. Joanna led the way, making
sure we had the best accommodations, the perfect views.

Spoleto

Along the way, she filled us in on the history of the castle, its recent renovation and new incarnation as a hotel. In the center of the complex of buildings—between the restaurant and the guest rooms—is an exquisite chapel that had been the family place of worship back in the Middle Ages.

"When the *comune* leased them the place and gave permission to do the renovation, they insisted that they restore this chapel. Now it's used for concerts, art shows, yoga classes—things like that."

Joanna stuck around, talking to Luca, while we unpacked and got comfortable. Then we all sat around a table on the terrace with a bottle of Grechetto, the local white wine, some olives, some almonds, a little cheese drizzled with *balsamica*—the Italians, it seems, never drink unless they're eating something. Joanna regaled us with a history of the valley, of Umbrans and Etruscans, of Popes and Holy Roman Emperors, of battles and sieges. It seems that pretty much everybody has occupied Spoleto over the centuries. After the fall of Rome, the Goths moved in for a while, then the Lombards (Germans). Perugia, its sister city just to the north, dominated it for a while, and then it was batted back and forth between the papacy and the Holy Roman Empire. Spoleto did have one notable moment of getting its back up in the third century B.C.—when the city stopped Hannibal in his tracks during his relentless march to Rome. Sitting on the terrace of the Castello, looking down on the valley, we could almost see and hear the clash of the armies below. This was after we cracked the second bottle of Grechetto.

Joanna talked about St. Francis, who lived and breathed in this valley back in the thirteenth century, and of his monumental effect on the church—and on the world in general. Her knowledge is encyclopedic and her delivery was a delightful mixture of cultures—a cross, perhaps, between Alistair Cooke and Jackie Mason. When she talked about St. Francis, it was more like gossip than history, which made it much more fun to listen to. St. Francis was a very complicated piece of work, and Joanna made sure we appreciated the entire spectrum of his personality.

When Jill is really entertained by somebody, she gets a wicked glint in her eye and her cheeks get rosy. That's what she looked like sitting on that terrace listening to Joanna's stories. Caroline, who has a very high tolerance for gossip and slander, was enchanted as well. And Joanna, clearly at home in the spotlight, sucked up the attention like a sponge. The more wine that went down, the more salacious her history became, until it seemed that the story of the relationship between the sainted Francis and Clare had been ripped from the pages of the *National Enquirer.*

"What about your history?" Jill asked her as we watched the setting sun turn the valley to gold. "How did you end up in this incredible place?"

"Well, I have a checkered past," she said with a raised eyebrow, "and I'm married to a very interesting man."

Joanna was born into the theater. Her father was Duncan Ross, a British actor/director who came over to the States around the time of the great American regional theater movement. Shortly after Tyrone Guthrie founded his seminal theater in Minneapolis, Duncan Ross went to the Seattle Repertory Theater, where he would become the artistic director. His daughter, Joanna, always the rebel, horrified her parents by spurning a university education and heading straight to New York to jump into the professional theater scene. She worked at Ellen Stewart's famous La Mama troupe for a while, and then moved on to the casting office at Joe Papp's Public Theater. That's around the time she met Bruce. Shortly after, they were married, and not long after that they had their son, Miles.

"Bruce can do anything—and has," she boasted. "When I met him, he was still doing some acting. He had been with La Mama from the beginning. That's how we first knew about Spoleto. The troupe came here on one of their European tours and Bruce fell totally in love with it.

"But then he figured he had to earn a living—being married with a kid and all—so he got into film editing, which he quickly mastered. That's about the time I got into the agent business. We were the classic successful New York couple. I was working twelve, fourteen hours a day; then I'd go home and read scripts all evening. Bruce was cutting commercials, which took up a huge amount of time as well. We never saw each other; we never had any time to spend with our kid; and after a few years of this we decided to chuck it all and move the whole family over here and start over.

"Bruce went back to school and got a degree in teaching

English as a second language—I told you, he can do anything. Now he's teaching English to the Italian Army, which sounds like the beginning of an old joke, but it's not."

"What about you?" asked Jill.

"I sell a little real estate on the side. You know, to people like you."

I nodded and said nothing. Jill smiled and shook her head. We all sat there quietly and took in the view, the setting sun and the warm feeling of the wine creeping up our spines and massaging our shoulders. After a moment, we asked Joanna if she'd like to join us for our farmhouse lunch the next day.

"Patrico? Sure. I'd never turn down a chance to go to Patrico."

Five

AN *AGRITURISMO* IS A BED-AND-BREAKFAST on a real working farm. They're all over Italy and, like anything else, there are good ones and bad ones. The idea—bolstered by some healthy tax incentives—is to encourage rural farmers to stay on their land and continue to farm it. It's an inducement offered by the government to preserve a way of life that's intrinsic to the culture and identity of Italy itself. Sometimes, an enterprising pseudo-farmer looking for a tax break will plant a few crops in the backyard, sex it all up to look like a working farm on paper and call it an *agriturismo*. But some are real farms that have been in the family for generations; they've been growing the crops, tending the animals, unearthing the truffles, harvesting the grapes for wine, distilling the wine for grappa for centuries. Such a place is the Agriturismo Bartoli in Patrico, which sits atop the sacred mountain of Monteluco.

We met Joanna at around eleven at a little gas station off the Flaminia and headed up toward Patrico. She told us to come early because there were lots of things to see along the way. We all piled into one car and let Joanna be our tour guide. She told us that Monteluco has always been considered a sacred mountain, since before history. Its name is derived from *Lucas,* which means holy wood. The Romans considered the ilex trees that still thrive here to be sacrosanct, and there's a sign from the third century A.D. describing—in Latin—the punishment for anyone who cut one of these trees. It was a stiff fine—it would've cost you a couple of oxen, at least. In the fifth century, Syrian monks fleeing persecution came to the mountain and lived in the tiny caves that you can still crawl through today. Then, in the early thirteenth century, St. Francis founded his first monastery here, which is still up and running. So the mountain fairly seethes with holiness.

We stopped at the monastery and went inside. There's a framed letter on the wall from Michelangelo written back in the fifteenth century and describing his stay at the monastery—the Italian version of George Washington slept here. As we were poking around, a young friar came out and asked us if we wanted to see the very chapel that St. Francis had prayed in every day. It was tiny—as, apparently, Francis was himself, though not so small that he didn't singlehandedly postpone the Reformation of the Catholic Church for four hundred years.

Then we got back in the car and drove to the very top of the mountain. Joanna told us to pull over at a promontory that jutted out over the farms below.

"Look over there. That's the whole Spoleto Valley. You see how wide it is—farms and such?"

We nodded.

"Then, look over this way. That's the Valnerina."

It had a totally different personality—wilder, narrower,

with heavily timbered hills plunging steeply down to the river Nera, which cuts through the valley floor on its way south, joins the Tiber and heads on into Rome. Beyond the valley we could see the snow-covered Apennines, the spine of Italy that makes its way along the whole length of the boot. Jill came up behind me and put her arms around my waist. She held me tightly for a long moment, gazing out over the two valleys. Umbria was getting to her.

We pulled into the Bartoli farm, which encompasses five hundred hectares at the top of the mountain. That's over twelve hundred acres.

The farm is a compound of stone buildings—some very old, some newer—perched here and there among the barns and corrals on the hillside. Caroline, who tends to be painfully shy in new situations, saw a pack of dogs fenced in above one of the barns and ran up to see them.

"Those are truffle dogs," said Joanna. "Worth their weight in gold."

Caroline found her way into their pen, knelt down and enjoyed a few minutes of unconditional love from eight or ten frantically licking puppies.

Outside the main house against one wall was a wooden bench, and seated on the bench, his eyes closed to the sun, was Domenico, grandpa and patriarch of the Bartoli family. He's ninety-six years old this year, and we learned from Joanna that when he was in his seventies he committed to memory the entire *Divine Comedy* of Dante, and he can still be called on to recite it on special occasions. There are newspaper articles on the wall inside attesting to this feat.

The dining room has two long tables—each one could seat at least twenty people—that were set with plates, glasses and silverware. Marcella, who is the mama of the family, the head cook, and clearly in charge of the operation, told us to sit anywhere we liked as the room quickly filled up with family, farmhands and other lucky souls who were either staying at the *agriturismo* or, like us, just catching lunch. There were probably about thirty of us all together.

The meal that followed was like no meal I had ever eaten. This was partly because of the place—the generous room in the solid stone house, straddling the precarious hillside, overlooking the two valleys, one green and wild, the other patchworked with farms. And it was because of the Bartoli family, who were as solidly grounded on the mountain as the stones they used to build their houses. And it was because of the food, every morsel of which was grown, raised, foraged, butchered, rendered or distilled right here on the farm. This is the most local culinary experience you can get.

First, plates of *salume* were placed, family style, on the tables, along with baskets of fresh, homemade bread. *Salume* means "assorted preserved meats"—salami, sausages, ham—that are hung in the cellar for a couple of years until they're aged to perfection. Plates of bruschetta followed, some topped with tomatoes and basil, some with a mixture of wild mushrooms and liver. Each table had two jeroboams of red wine—unlabeled—that continued to circulate, faster and faster as the meal progressed.

Then came the pasta—family style, of course. Handmade *strongozzi,* which is the local dried pasta in this part of Umbria, in a wild boar sauce that had been slow-cooked for hours until the sweet, pungent flesh of the pig melted into the onions, celery, carrots and tomatoes to form a thick ragu that fairly clung to the al dente strands of pasta. A second helping was offered, and I felt it was my duty as a guest to accept.

We talked and laughed, attempting to communicate with family and guests in our fumbling Italian. Joanna helped a lot. She is fairly fluent with the language, though she makes no attempt at all to try to sound like an Italian. She served as the United Nations simultaneous interpreter, barking explanations in both directions at once and sounding—in either language—like the British-born New York talent agent that she is.

The *secondi* was chicken with truffles, served with plates and plates of just-harvested vegetables and potatoes. Never in my life has chicken tasted like this. The deep, powerful, almost gamy taste reached up and grabbed our taste buds by the collar as if to say, "This is chicken, buster." And the truffles were . . . well, truffles.

Then, a *dolce,* a simple cake with bowls of berries. And then cheese—a pecorino. It seems the sheep are let out into the high meadow to eat the wildflowers when they come into bloom in the early spring. And this cheese was made of the milk that comes from that happy occurrence. Cheese is considered a *digestivo* in Italy, to make everything go down in the proper way.

After lunch, Caroline made her way back to play with the dogs, Jill stood out on the hill, looking at the vista, and Joanna and I went into the bar to be served an espresso by Felice, Marcella's husband and padrone of the establishment.

"Don't ask for cappuccino after ten o'clock in the morning," said Joanna. "Only espresso. If you order cappuccino after ten, they'll think you're a German."

We joined up with Jill and Caroline outside by the barn and I asked Joanna how to go about paying for lunch.

"Just find Felice and ask him how much."

Even I knew that much Italian, so I went back to the bar to pay up. He asked me how many we were and I told him four. He wrote down a figure in euros that, when converted, came to about fifteen bucks a head, wine and tip—and truffles—included.

I went into the kitchen to thank Marcella and the others for cooking so brilliantly and I noticed that she had prepared the entire lunch—for thirty people—on a tiny old four-burner stove. At home, if I don't have my six-burner Viking with a grill in the middle, I find it quite impossible to cook a dinner for eight.

As we were driving back down the mountain, Joanna asked us if we'd like to take a quick tour of Spoleto. We had nothing else to do but digest our lunch, so we said we would. About a mile before we reached the bottom and the Via Flaminia, she directed us to turn off onto a dirt lane not

Marcella in the kitchen at Patrico

much wider than the car. We parked and followed her up the trail. About two hundred yards along, we found ourselves on the Monteluco side of the Ponte delle Torre, the ancient aqueduct that connects the hill town of Spoleto to the sacred mountain. As we walked across, taking in the splendid view of the valley below, Joanna caught us up on the history of the town, the aqueduct and La Rocca, the medieval fortress that protects the Spoleto side of the bridge.

We meandered through the narrow, twisty cobblestone streets to the Piazza Mercato, where there's an ongoing farmers' market in the center of the square, and Joanna suggested we get some gelato.

"Italians follow a very strict code when it comes to eating, and one hard-and-fast rule is gelato at four o'clock. It's sort of a law. For me it's pistachio—but that's not legislated."

Jill tried the *frutta di bosco,* and Caroline got two flavors, one on top of the other—chocolate below and vanilla yogurt on top. I had *straciatella,* which is the Italian version of vanilla chocolate-chip. We felt very law-abiding, scarfing down our four o'clock gelatos as we walked over to the Cathedral Square.

The Spoleto Cathedral is a knockout—especially the initial approach to it. We walked along a narrow street from the Piazza Mercato and came to a wide descending staircase, at the bottom of which is the vast piazza that frames the cathedral. Because you're above it looking down, you can see the rolling hills of Umbria behind it—just like the backgrounds for so many of those frescoes by Giotto, Lippi and Signorelli.

"Okay," barked Joanna. "Spoleto Cathedral—five things." She bounded through the enormous doors and into the dark church. We scurried to keep up with her.

"I can't tell you how many times I've given this fucking tour over the last twelve years, so I've got it down. Five things."

She ticked them off on her fingers.

"The Lippi frescoes behind the altar, the random brick design on the floor, the gift from Barbarossa, the framed letter from St. Francis and the circular Rose Window above the entrance. We can see all five of them and be out of here in fifteen minutes. And you'll know more about the cathedral than most Spoletini."

Sure enough, fifteen minutes later—well, maybe twenty—we were back out in the bright sunlight of the piazza, having digested a succinct but thoroughly educational description of each of the five cathedral highlights. Our tour guide was nothing short of brilliant.

"What about that wooden cross?" asked Caroline.

"What about it?"

"Well, you said five things; wouldn't that be six?"

Joanna shrugged.

"Yeah, okay. Six things. Can you get me back to my car? I have to pick Bruce up at the train station."

As we dropped her at her car at the gas station, I asked her if she had any properties that were available for sale. "We're not buying. So, don't show us anything if that's a problem. I'm just curious what's available."

She barely blinked. "How about tomorrow? I can call around and see if there's anything good."

"We have to leave around noon—we're driving down to Sorrento."

"Lucky you. I'll give you a call tonight and we'll make a plan."

Six

I REALLY WASN'T LOOKING TO BUY; I had made a solemn promise to Jill. I just wanted to check out the lay of the land—see what things were going for. I wanted to compare it with France. Hey, I'm a property junkie. When I'm on the road, on a job or just traveling, you can always find me scanning the listings in some real estate window, checking out the deals. And it's a great way to see the countryside—you know, to get away from all the touristy stuff.

And that, your honor, is the case for the defense.

JoJo—for that, we learned from Luca, is what Joanna is called by her friends—met us for breakfast at the hotel. We had already checked out and put the bags in the car. I very much wanted to get on the road at a reasonable hour. We were going to have to skirt Rome, navigate through Naples and then get on a tiny, crowded road that would take us into Sorrento. I definitely didn't want to hit Naples at rush hour.

"I have two places to show you," said JoJo over coffee on the terrace. "And maybe a third if my friend Bruno ever calls me back. Why don't you follow me, and when we're done you can get straight on the highway and be on your way."

First, we saw a nice little new construction that sat in the middle of somebody's farm, on the way up to Montefalco. The house was completed except for the finishes—we would get to choose the flooring, the appliances, the paint job, etc.—and you could tell it was going to be a very nice house. And the price really got my attention. Even with all the work yet to be done, it was clear that Umbria was a much better deal than France or Tuscany. But it sat literally in the middle of a farm—with deeded access along a skinny little road that bumped through somebody else's property. And it was kind of stuck out there in the middle of everything, without trees.

When we got to the second place—which was a tight, uncomfortable little redo in the beautiful hill town of Campello Alto—JoJo took us aside for a conference.

"I spoke to Bruno and he says he'll show you the house. Now, I have to tell you I think you're gonna love this place; I'm pretty sure of that. But I should be straight with you that, first of all, Bruno's a good friend of mine. Second, he's asking what I would consider a high price for it—fair, but high. I have to tell you that. He's been threatening to put it on the market for a couple of years, and up to now, he—and Mayes, his wife—have been reluctant to let it go.

"Let's see it."

"I think you're going to like this house."

We turned off a two-lane country road onto a dirt track that cut through two large groves of olive trees. The road trickled down a couple hundred yards to an electric gate. JoJo pushed the bell, the gate opened for us and we drove into a secluded acre planted with fruit trees—we later learned there was plum, apricot, pear, almond, apple and fig—and, most prominently, 125 olive trees in various stages of development. There was a spacious parking area and steps that led us up to a cozy two-story stone house, covered with vines. Every window had boxes filled with red geraniums. Just outside the entrance to the kitchen was a vine-covered pergola with a table and chairs, and sitting there were Bruno and Mayes.

"You have to excuse us," said Mayes in a lilting Spanish accent that caught us completely off guard. Mayes is from Mexico City. "We're cleaning up after the renters."

"We've been using the house as a rental for the last couple of years," said Bruno, whose Italian accent was diluted by his years of living in the States—both in New York and Los Angeles.

"So, we come and spend the day, have lunch. You know, we love this place," said Mayes.

"Yeah, my mom is in the kitchen right now making lunch—so, if you want to stay . . ."

We all blurted out thanks and explained that we really had to get on the road shortly.

"Where ya goin'?" asked Bruno.

We told him about our trip and the birthday party that we were headed to in Puglia and they said that they go to Puglia all the time for quick vacations. Mayes offered us some water, and we pulled up chairs and made ourselves comfortable under the pergola.

It turned out that they're both in the movie business— Bruno is a production designer with an Academy Award nomination on his resume, and Mayes is a very busy and successful costume designer. They met when Bruno was doing a movie in Mexico. She's a beauty. Her long, curly hair was tied back, revealing a wide face, bright hazel eyes and cheek-bones that go on forever.

Bruno I fell for instantly. He's at ease with himself, charmingly self-deprecating, a great storyteller. He's a Roman, and has the cockiness—some would say the arrogance—that's often attributed to people who grow up in the Italian capital. His eyes are in a perennial state of amusement and they seem to be constantly scanning the horizon for fun. And he's about my size and shape—which makes him fairly perfect.

"So, you guys want to buy our house, huh?"

"Our little Rustico," said Mayes, wistfully, for that's what they call the place.

"Well, I don't know about that, but . . ."

"You want to come in and take a look?"

We entered into the kitchen, where, indeed, there was Bruno's mom sautéing some zucchini on the range.

"This is some actress, right? You hired her when you heard we were coming over."

We shook hands with Mama, who explained—in Italian—that she loves to come up from Rome and cook for Bruno and Mayes whenever there's a changeover at the house. She, too, loves the Rustico.

The house was tiny—kitchen and living/dining room on the first floor; two bedrooms, each with a full bath, on the second. And that's it. But it was perfect, to my eye. It was about 350 years old but had all the modern conveniences, subtly added so as not to disturb its history. Bruno's a set designer—he knows what he's doing. When we went back outside, he pointed out the wood-burning oven next to the pergola. It was huge. I thought it was a guesthouse.

"The *forno* is four hundred years old. It was here before the house."

"Does it still work?"

"Oh yeah. We had a party here last summer and made pizzas for thirty people."

That did it. They had me. I was theirs.

"Tell 'em about the plans," put in JoJo.

"Oh yeah, we have approved plans from the *comune* to put on an addition, to roughly double the size of the house. Also a pool. It's not easy to get plans to build approved these days. Especially in the olive groves."

Bruno got out the plans and we all gathered around the table to look at them. Mayes went into the kitchen and brought out some wine. The bottle was one of those refillable ones with a rubber stopper—no label. Mama brought out the platter of zucchini and they insisted that we relax and have something to eat and drink. Tomatoes from the garden appeared—plus sliced mozzarella, drizzled with olive oil, and some bread to sop it all up with. We were laughing, telling stories about movie shoots in foreign places; Mayes wanted to know all about Caroline's life, growing up in Asia. The minutes slipped by unnoticed. The sun was now hitting the pergola from a whole different angle.

Jill was in the middle of telling a story about our movie experience in Italy twenty-five years ago with Lina Wertmuller.

"Wasn't Giannini in that?" asked Bruno.

"Yeah," I said. "We've known Giancarlo for a long time."

Bruno picked up his cell phone and dialed.

"Giancarlo? Bruno. I got a guy here says he knows you."

And he handed me the phone. I hadn't actually seen Giancarlo for twenty years.

"Giancarlo? *Sono Mikey* [pronounced "Meekie"—which is what all the Italians on the movie called me]."

"Mikey? What the hell you are doing there?" he said in his still terrible English.

"Maybe I'm buying Bruno's house."

"Rustico? He's not selling Rustico. They love this place. Tell him I said he is *pazzo*. *Tutto pazzo*."

After we hung up I told Bruno that Giancarlo said he was crazy. Bruno's puckish face jutted out from under the brim of his baseball cap.

"He's probably right."

He and Mayes were holding hands under the table. There was a long pause as we soaked up the energy of the Rustico; then Mayes spoke.

"A couple of weeks ago, we were sitting out here. The sun was setting. And I pointed out to Bruno that the vines had finally grown together at the top of the pergola. The next day he called JoJo and talked to her about putting the house on the market. If I only realized what I was doing, I would have sneaked out in the middle of the night and cut them back."

"What's next—you know?" said Bruno with a grin. "I have to be building something. Otherwise you die."

I looked over at Jill, and she smiled back. And then she nodded to me. Not just a nod—she pursed her lips and furrowed her brow as if to say, "I've thought this over very carefully and I'm about to give you my considered opinion," and then she closed her eyes and shot me an emphatic, single, eloquent nod. And I felt the earth move.

Seven

WE HUGGED BRUNO AND MAYES and said our good-byes; we told them that we were interested but had to talk it over. We asked them if Bruno's mom came with the deal because that would certainly enhance the package. We hugged Bruno's mom. Then we hugged JoJo and thanked her for being our guide over the last few days. We're actors; we hug. The electric gate opened to let us out and our car slowly climbed the hill back to the main road, leaving behind the Rustico and those wonderful people.

My heart was pounding. Was Jill's sudden reversal making me nervous? Maybe all my talk about buying a place in Europe had been nothing more than a bluff and she—with a nod—had just called it. A thousand doubts flooded my mind. Can we really afford this? We barely work anymore—the fact that we can spend so much time in Italy is a testament to that. Am I being a fool to spend a healthy chunk of our life savings on a place so far away? And what will my brother say? Oh, God. My brother, Ed, is four years older than me and represents the more sober side of the family. Well, maybe "sober" isn't exactly the right word, but he's our accountant and financial adviser and I use him as a guardrail for whenever I round a particularly emotional curve. It's a gift having an older brother who looks out for you, but I could already envision the argument we would get into over this one. And was that really a nod Jill gave me back there or did she just have something in her eye?

Jill's being on board for this adventure is not merely a piece of the puzzle; it's the whole deal. After years of energetically, passionately, doggedly chasing my own pleasure, I've come to realize that the only way for me to be truly satisfied is to give Jill everything she wants. Which doesn't mean, by the way, that I don't get to have my own dreams. She loves my dreams; they've often led us to fabulous times together. But if I get my eye so firmly fixed on the dream that I take it off her—even for a second—then I've blown the deal.

No, she definitely nodded to me back there under the pergola. She'd seemed to be saying that she wanted this. Why the change? Why this house? Why this moment?

"Because it felt like home," said Jill simply, from the passenger seat.

Wait a minute. Was I talking out loud or was she reading my mind again?

"All those other places—in the south of France—they were vacation places. It was fun to go there for a week or two, but we could really live our lives in this house."

I started shaking again. This was really happening.

"Can we afford it?" she asked.

"Not really."

"Well . . . that's okay."

And it was.

We were approaching Rome and the Grand Raccordo Annulare, which is the highway that circles the city. I took the exit heading south to Naples. All I could think of was that the Rustico was getting farther and farther away.

That night I called JoJo and let her know we were really interested. I told her I needed to run it by my brother. I told her that the dollar/euro exchange rate was particularly bad at the moment and I might want to wait a month or two until it calmed down. I asked her to find out how much Bruno and Mayes made from renting it out. This might make it easier to propose the whole idea to my brother—more like a business venture. I could just see Ed's eyes roll when I tried that one.

As I drifted off to sleep that night I ran images of the Rustico over and over on the screen behind my eyes—the little rooms, the pergola, the *forno,* the olive trees.

Sorrento was a bore. English tearooms and T-shirt shops. My mind was in Umbria. I couldn't focus on anything else. Except for the day we took a ferry into Naples and walked for two hours through the chaotic streets to search for the best pizza in the world. We found it; we tried it; it *was* the best pizza in the world—in a pizzeria called Trianon on the Via Colletta. I couldn't stop eating; I was in an altered state. The crust—charred, but still a little chewy; the sauce—fresh San Marzano tomatoes right from where they were invented; the sausage (because I love sausage on my pizza) filled with the taste of real Italian pork, so different from its tasteless American counterpart; mozzarella made from the milk of buffalo who were grazing right outside the window (well, you know—fresh). And the oven, which burned wood to temperatures of up to 1200 degrees, galvanized these tastes together into a hot, chewy, slightly crunchy masterpiece. The only problem was that the people sharing the table with us said that there was another place across the street called Michele's that was even better. I tried to enlist Jill and Caroline in a bulimic ritual so that we could all have a second lunch, but they dragged me, kicking and screaming, back to the ferry.

JoJo called the next day with all kinds of news. Bruno and Mayes asked if we wanted to drive back and stay in the house—just to get a feel for it. It wasn't being rented out that week and they would be happy for us to be their guests. It seems they wanted us to be the ones who bought it. Bruno also offered a break on the price—he'd base the cost on a more reasonable dollar/euro conversion. Then Caroline chirped up with an offer to buy in for a share of the house. She, too, was caught up in the spell of the Rustico. Also, her adopted dad lives in Zurich and she liked the idea of having a base on this side of the Atlantic. Everything seemed to be lining up in favor of our buying the house.

The next day we left Campania and headed across the lower part of the Italian Peninsula toward Puglia. Birgit had arranged for us to stay in a bed-and-breakfast in a little town called Maritimma, which was all the way down near the southernmost tip of the heel of the boot of Italy. We were to stay in a convent that had been converted, Birgit told us, by Lord and Lady McAlpine. They were to be our hosts, which made me a little uncomfortable. It all sounded very starchy and proper and not at all conducive to the mood of our laid-back, Italian adventure. Birgit argued that they were very nice people, but the fact is Birgit can get a little starchy herself.

Then we got lost. The farther south we drove, the worse the signs were. We lost what highway there was and found

COURTESY OF THE AUTHOR

Pizza in Naples

ourselves dumped onto a country lane that puttered its way through an endless string of tiny bleach-white villages. And in every town, at the main piazza, there would be a pole with a list of arrows, pointing in various directions and providing the names of towns and the number of kilometers it would take to reach them. And none of the towns were on our map. Not one. And at the bottom of the list would be an arrow that said, "*Tutte le direzione,*" which means, obviously, all directions, and every time we followed that sign, we hit a dead end. In Puglia, all roads lead to nowhere.

It was now late in the day, and we were hot and thirsty and seemingly no closer to Maritimma than we had been hours before. Caroline started snarling from the backseat. This is something she does when her blood sugar drops. Jill, too, was getting testy. I, of course, was the target of both their bad moods. We argued about whether to stop and get something to eat, but finally we decided to grit our collective teeth and just get there.

We finally stumbled onto Maritimma and checked our instructions from Birgit. She said the convent was on the road as you head out of town toward Castro Marina. By a miracle we found a sign that had that name on it—with an arrow and everything. We pulled up to an old church that we thought must be the place and I parked the car across the street from the chapel.

"Oh my God, there are dead people!"

Indeed there was an old cemetery next to where our car was parked. Caroline was having none of it.

"I'm not sleeping next to dead people. Call Birgit. We'll find another place."

Jill tried to explain to Caroline that these dead people wouldn't hurt her, that they had been dead a very long time, but I knew this was just the blood sugar talking. I left them and went to find the convent, which I assumed was on the other side of the church. As I approached the door, it magically opened to greet me and a beautiful young woman in a white diaphanous dress with antique silver chains falling around her hips spoke to me in an impeccable British accent. "Mr. Tucker? We've been expecting you."

I followed her inside—I would have followed her anywhere—and it was as if I had fallen into a dream. The inner courtyard was like a Moorish castle, elegantly decorated with antiques, richly colored carpets on the walls and floors, oceans of deep pillows to sit on, and a low round table filled with fresh figs, cheeses, raw vegetables (a specialty of Puglia), breads, cakes, a pot of herbal tea and decanters of enticing, cool, fruity liquids.

"Leave your bags in the car and come sit and unwind."

I gestured that I would find the ladies and be right back. I saw them standing over by the dead people and I waved to them to come over.

"Caroline really doesn't want to stay here, honey."

I waved again.

"You're not going to believe this. Come on!"

Something in my tone got their attention and they walked across the road, shooting me hateful glances.

An hour later we were sprawled out on pillows, sipping a lovely local white wine, deep in conversation with Alistair and Athena McAlpine, who weren't starchy in the least. Alistair McAlpine is one of the world's great collectors: of antiques, paintings, sculpture, furniture, books, manuscripts—and beautiful wives. He had been treasurer in Margaret Thatcher's government and a master fund-raiser for the Conservatives. He wrote a book about those experiences titled, *Once a Jolly Bag Man*. Never had I so enjoyed a Conservative.

Athena is Greek, but educated in London. She is the most relaxed, elegant and thoughtful hostess one could ever hope for. By our beds were books hand-selected by Athena that she'd guessed might be of interest to each of us. She'd guessed right in every case.

Now that we were properly and comfortably housed, we approached the birthday week with renewed energy. Birgit is a master organizer, and she had us hopping all over this extraordinary region of Italy, with parties every night and sightseeing every day. The highlight was an outdoor party at a wonderful inn way out in the country. It was a night of dancing—featuring the tarantella, which is danced to the folk music of Puglia, called *pizzica-pizzica*. To start the dancing, a young woman with long curly hair, a flowing skirt and bare feet demonstrated the tarantella on the cool stone floor of the patio. She was irresistible. Soon we were all up and dancing on into the night.

Birgit's Italian friends were eager to advise us about buying real estate in Italy. They thought we were lucky to have found Bruno's place. Apparently an old stone cottage that's been renovated, that's private and that sits on a nice piece of land is what everyone is looking for. I called JoJo every evening before dinner, working out various scenarios. Finally, I told her that we'd have to wait until we got back to the States before we made a final decision. I needed to run it through the older-brother test, and I also thought it would be better to be away and out from under the spell of Italy before I committed myself to anything I might regret.

The night we got back to California, I nervously called my brother and spilled the whole story to him. Without the slightest pause, he said, "We'll take the last two weeks in September. Does it have a pool?"

Eight

Two weeks later I was flying across the ocean—on my own—to buy the house. JoJo, who was quickly becoming invaluable, had set up everything in advance of my arrival. She had instructed me to hand-carry certified checks that would allow me to open an Italian bank account, purchase the house and pay the *notaio,* who would give the law's blessing to our transaction. She set up an appointment for me to get a *codice fiscale,* which is the Italian equivalent of a social security number. She had found me the best deal on home owner's insurance. She'd transferred the billing for gas, electric, water and phone into my name. All of this is part of the deal when you buy a house through JoJo.

I was too excited to sleep on the flight over. I was a man on a mission. The only flight I could get on such short notice had me changing planes in Amsterdam, with a four-hour layover. I toyed with the idea of checking my bag and heading to the nearest "coffee shop" to try a little legal marijuana, but then I remembered the few hundred thousand dollars of certified checks in my pocket and thought better of it. I found a little commuter airline that was leaving for Rome immediately and managed to get myself on it.

Since I was carrying very little—it was only a three-day trip—I sped through customs and immigration, got my rental car and was heading to Umbria by about two o'clock. The plan was to call JoJo on my cell phone when I reached Spoleto and she would meet me at the house to open the gate. I would be spending that night in the house—as a guest of Bruno and Mayes—and the next morning we would all meet at the *notaio* to transfer the title.

On the drive up, I tried to picture the house as I remembered it on that first day. We hadn't been able to take Bruno up on his offer to come back and stay there, and I realized I hadn't really paid attention to any of the details. I had been swept up in the general romantic feeling of the Rustico and had never checked things like water pressure, signs of termites, leaks, settling—all the things you're supposed to look for when you buy a house. I couldn't remember where the steps were to get upstairs. Was there a window on that far wall in the living room? Was there any light in the living room? Did the fireplace work? Well, I thought, I have this afternoon and tonight to check it out. I could still back out. Suddenly, the cold wind of doubt blew up my pant leg. I shivered. It was at least 90 degrees outside.

Also, there was an issue over the building permit for the addition. I had asked JoJo to make sure I had the actual permit in my hand before we signed the papers and, after some frantic e-mails back and forth between Bruno, the architect, the *comune,* JoJo and me, no one had yet been able to assure me that I would have it in time for the signing. This could be a real problem.

JoJo had stocked the house a bit—a bottle of Grechetto

in the fridge, some cheese and salami, some ground coffee, sugar and cream for the morning.

"I thought we'd meet you for dinner tonight at the Palazzaccio. You'll get to meet Bruce. The best thing for you is to stay up this afternoon, come out and have a great dinner, drink some wine, and get to sleep as late as you can stand it. That way you'll turn it around quicker."

She told me how to get to the Palazzaccio, which was a trattoria down on the Flaminia about ten minutes away. She said it was their favorite place—a kind of hangout for the expat community that made up their circle of friends.

"Have a nice afternoon," she said, and clapped me on the shoulder with a reassuring smile.

"Oh, and I think we have the building permit. Martin, the architect, is at the *comune* this afternoon and I'm pretty sure he'll be able to walk away with it. If not? Hey, you'll have a three-day vacation in Italy."

And with that, she left so that the Rustico and I could spend a little one-on-one time together.

I flushed the toilets, ran the hot water, checked the lights—all that kind of stuff. It was as solid as a rock. I climbed the steep wooden stairway from the kitchen to the bedrooms. Our room was to be the bigger one to the left. There's one step up from the wooden landing onto the brick-tiled floor of the bedroom and the bricks—the *pianelle*—had been worn down by God-knows-how-many years of footfalls on that step. It was U-shaped from wear. I couldn't get over that. I sat on the bed and stared at the doorway for a long time, thinking about the history of the little house, sitting in the middle of this field, surrounded by miles of olive trees in every direction.

I drove down to the Palazzaccio around eight-thirty. JoJo

and her husband, Bruce, were sitting outside in the back of the restaurant at a long picnic table with Martin—the architect who had done the design for Bruno—and his wife, Karen.

"Tomorrow morning, before we head into town for all the legal stuff, I arranged for Martin to meet us at the Rustico for a little meeting," JoJo said.

"Did we get the permit?"

"Not yet—but tomorrow, for sure," said Martin, a little nervously. "I'll bring it when we meet in the morning."

I explained that we weren't sure we wanted to get into a whole construction thing anyway—that maybe the house was perfect the way it was now.

"Why don't we talk about it tomorrow," said Martin, who, although he comes from Germany, is perfectly fluent in English as well as Italian. "Tonight is to relax, have a nice dinner and get a good night's sleep."

"The Palazzaccio is a typical family-run Umbrian trattoria, Michael," said Bruce quietly from the other side of the table. He seemed as quiet and contained as JoJo is outspoken and brash.

"About thirty-five years ago, Paolo was a truck driver who loved to entertain his friends. His wife was, and still is, a wonderful cook, and he had the kind of personality and generosity of spirit that regularly pulled in a large and fun-loving crowd. Eventually, they opened up this place and served simple food and local wine to other truck drivers and their families—and the Palazzaccio was born. Now their three daughters run the place, and you can't find a more honest meal."

Danila, one of the daughters, brought menus out and everyone started making recommendations as to what they thought I should eat. *Ravioli Letizia*—named after one of the granddaughters—was a specialty, filled with an eggplant mixture and sauced with tomato; so was *ravioli carciofi,* made with the fresh artichokes that were just arriving in the local markets.

"But if you've never had *strongozzi tartufo,* there's no better place to try it than here," said Bruce.

"Then maybe some lamb—you like lamb?" asked JoJo.

I nodded.

"Have the *castrato.* Don't be put off by the name—it's lamb grilled over wood; very simple and good. And have the fried potatoes—they're the best in the world."

"We'll get an order of the spinach as well—for the table," said Karen. She's an American, a modern dancer who had her own company in Philadelphia. I asked her what had brought them to this little area of Umbria and she explained that they, too, had been searching for the perfect place to start their new life together. Martin had heard that because of the damage from the great Umbrian earthquake in the late eighties, there was a dire need for architects in the area. Like JoJo and Bruce, their move to Umbria had involved a reinvention of themselves—both as people and as artists.

We ordered tons of food—they wanted me to try everything. Bottles of water—some with bubbles, some without—were brought to the table, along with carafes of wine—*rosso* and *bianco*—that were drawn from huge vats that stood in the backyard. There were toddlers chasing a family of kittens around the outdoor patio, older kids doing homework at another table, a baby clinging to her mama's dress as she carried food out from the kitchen. The other tables started to fill up—Italians don't even think about having

Nicola and Danila welcoming us to the Palazzaccio

dinner until nine o'clock at the earliest. Our table's conversation bounced easily from American politics to Italian politics to a history of the expat community here in the valley—which really started with Bruce when he came to the Spoleto Festival in the early sixties as an actor with La Mama.

The pasta came and everyone insisted I try everything. And as wonderful as the various ravioli were, the *strongozzi tartufo* was a veritable revelation.

Strongozzi—or *strangozzi*—is a round noodle, a little thicker than spaghetti, with a more handmade feeling to it than the pasta you find in a box. It's the local choice in this part of Umbria. In this dish, it's tossed in the best olive oil, which has been flavored with a chopped clove of garlic and a chopped anchovy, then liberally showered with fresh-grated black truffles. That's it. You should use enough garlic-laced oil so that there's a little pool of it left in the bowl when the last al dente strand of pasta has been scarfed down. This you mop up with a piece of traditional unsalted Umbrian bread. Ideally, you should have a little trace of the oil still visible on your chin by the time the *secondi* arrive. This indicates a properly eaten bowl of *strongozzi tartufo*.

Grilled lamb was next for me, along with the spinach with garlic and the fried potatoes. Then a salad, some cheese and, finally, grappa. By the third glass of this lethal potion, I felt I had known these people for years. Karen and Martin told a story about how their gas man had backed his delivery truck over the cliff when he'd tried to turn around on their very precarious road. And Bruce became mellower, more loquacious, with each refilling of the grappa glass. He gave an elegant lecture, I believe, on the various species of birds in the Yucatán. JoJo was in deep Italian conversation with Danila about their respective children and the differences between Italian and American kids. And I actually understood them. The more grappa I drank, the better was my comprehension. I felt I was ready to run for the Italian parliament by the time we teetered out of there.

They all walked me to my car and I carefully made my way up the dark country road and back to the Rustico. Minutes later I fell into the old iron bed that stood on the ancient brick tiles and slept like a migrant worker.

Nine

WE BOUGHT OUR LITTLE HOUSE IN ITALY in pretty much the same way we'd done everything else in our life together—hand in hand, headlong over the falls in a barrel, and then on the way down looking at each other and wondering whether this was really a good idea.

We arrived at Rome's Leonardo da Vinci Airport—known to the locals as Fiumicino—on the first of September for a six-week get-acquainted stay in our new, very old house. We had stuffed our suitcases with pots and pans, bed linens, silverware, picture frames—I don't know why I thought I wouldn't be able to find cooking implements in Italy, where they have been known to cook every now and then. I guess I wanted the security of my familiar sauté pans, knives and spatulas.

Our son, Max, had been traveling through Europe with a friend and they met us at the airport. They had just been in Barcelona for a week and Max was eager to check out what his crazy parents were doing. He liked the idea of having a place to crash in Europe. Max is a jazz drummer and his friend, Isaac, is a guitarist. They had been checking out the opportunities for jamming in Amsterdam, Paris and Barcelona, where there's a much wider audience for jazz than there is in the States. With their backpacks, Isaac's guitar and our excessive luggage we had to trade up for a larger car—a station wagon, which wasn't really big enough either. It was a stick shift with a propensity to stall coming out of first gear. With severely limited rear vision because of the bags piled up in the back, we coughed and sputtered our way onto the highway and headed north.

Two hours later, when we turned off the main road, bumped down the little rutted path to our front gate and drove into the Rustico, all the tensions and anxieties that I had been carrying drifted away in the warm breeze that wafted through the olive trees. The boys jumped out of the car and parked themselves at the table under the pergola as if waiting for someone to serve them lunch. Jill went right to the *orto,* the vegetable garden Bruno and Mayes had planted and graciously maintained for us to enjoy. There were still vines of cherry tomatoes, zucchini, beans, hot and sweet peppers, *rucola* and big, bushy bunches of basil.

I started unloading the car and hauling the luggage into the house. I wrestled with the lock on the *persiani,* the heavy wooden shutters that covered all the doors and windows, and finally got myself into the kitchen. There, in the middle of the floor, were eight giant cardboard boxes that we'd shipped over the month before. More pots and pans, exercise equipment, blankets and comforters, underwear and socks, hiking boots. We had a lot of unpacking to do.

That's when the idea of garbage came up. What do we do with it? Do they pick it up? Do they recycle? Do they separate? Does some guy come by in a truck? The house is way out in the middle of nowhere. And if he does come by with a truck, how do I know which day?

Garbage is big for a guy. I think it goes way back, maybe all the way to the hunter/gatherer time. You gather; there's garbage. And you can be damn sure the little cave woman isn't going to help you schlep anything out to the curb. I called JoJo.

"No. Nobody's gonna come by and pick up the garbage. You take it to these bins—they're all over the place, you can't miss 'em. Green for bottles, blue for plastic, gray for everything else. Just take it with you every time you leave the house."

All right. Cool. They recycle, they separate—this is not an alien planet, after all. I felt a tingle of imminent masculine achievement coursing through my loins. Yes, my Italian was limited to words like "pencil" and "banana"; admittedly I lacked the courage to venture out into the passing lane on the autostrada—but I knew where our garbage was going, and that was enough to awaken in me a sense of competence, of leadership, of, dare I say, power? Garbage is big.

I did a reconnoiter. While Jill was putting the clothes away in tiny wardrobes that tried to pass for closets, I snuck out in the car to pin down the location of our bins. And they were everywhere! About a mile down the road, just off to the side next to a field was a gray one. That's for food scraps and the like. But a little farther down—right as I got to our little village—was a veritable gold mine. A blue one, a green one and two gray ones—all lined up on the back side of the church, which, by the way, dates all the way back to the thirteenth century. This was the place. This was my local.

When I got back to the house to announce my discovery,

I found Max and Isaac zonked out on the couch in the living room. For the past three weeks, they had been on a strict regimen of partying and club hopping and then using the daylight hours—much like vampires—to regenerate themselves. I'd just gone into the kitchen and opened one of the boxes containing my beloved pots and pans in order to get them organized when I heard Jill's voice calling from the bedroom upstairs.

"Honey, could you help me for a minute?"

I climbed the tiny stairs from the kitchen, taking care not to bump my head on the steel girder cleverly tucked behind the ancient wooden beam that made the kitchen so authentically seventeenth century. Bruno had subtly retrofitted the whole cottage for earthquakes. That we were now splitting our time between Northern California and Umbria, two of the world's more active fault areas, seemed somehow appropriate.

Jill was making up our bed and wanted me to help. As I fitted the corner of the bottom sheet onto my side of the mattress, I felt her eyes on me. I looked up and saw she had that expression on her face—the one that said we weren't just making the bed, we were *making the bed*.

"How many houses now?" she asked softly.

And we both started to count silently the places we had lived, the beds we had made together since that first little apartment in Washington, D.C.

"I get twelve," she said finally.

"No. This is thirteen."

We went over them all together and I reminded her of our first New York apartment—the sublet on East Fifth Street where we had to step over the drug addicts on the front step to get into the lobby.

"Right," she said. "Thirteen."

I tiptoed downstairs to make sure the boys were properly passed out. Then we quietly closed our bedroom door and gave the bed a little trial run—just to make sure it worked properly.

Later that afternoon, when we had finished the major unpacking, Jill and the boys helped me pile all our trash into the back of our station wagon so that on our way to the supermarket we could make our first ceremonial dump. The road into town from our house is a narrow two-way country lane, but when it reaches the church at the edge of town, it separates—one-way to the right of the church and, coming up from the other side of town, one-way against us to the left. And connecting them along the back side of the church is a twenty-yard-long gravel road—also one-way against us. That's where the garbage cans are. So to get to them properly, we would have to drive around the church, all the way out of town, circle around to the left, drive back through town, pass the church and hang a left.

Or, I figured, we could just turn in—against the one-way sign, quickly drop off the garbage, make a U-turn, and nobody'd be the wiser. We hadn't seen more than two cars in town since we'd arrived.

I pulled in, commanded the boys to open the trunk and start unloading the garbage—green for glass, blue for plastic, gray for everything else—while I kept a lookout for cars. The boys moved slowly—passive-aggressively slowly, I thought—refusing to comprehend the need for haste. And, sure enough, a car came around the church signaling to make a left and there was no room to let him by. I might have been able to move to the side a bit but the boys had left both doors open, so I smiled and shrugged helplessly at my new neighbor, and screamed for the boys to pick up the pace.

Then, another car pulled up behind the first one, its signal also insistently blinking. Now the road was actually tied up. I had created perhaps the only traffic jam in the history of Central Umbria. I looked in panic over my shoulder and saw Max putting one plastic bottle at a time into the slot. And Isaac was neatly folding cardboard as if he were wrapping a Mother's Day present.

Then a third car got in line, its blinker in tandem with the other two. And they had all turned their lights on as if in silent protest against my civic indiscretion. Finally the boys finished and leisurely got back into the car. I couldn't go forward because of the guy in front of me, and when I backed up to make a three-point turn so as to be facing the right direction, all the cars ceremoniously passed me, staring daggers through my windshield. I sheepishly pulled in line behind them and noticed that there were four or five cars more—all with their lights on—getting in line behind me.

"It's a funeral, honey," offered Jill.

"Great."

"Maybe you should turn your lights on."

We made our way—funereally—through town, heading to the Flaminia. I tried to keep my head down and drive at the same time. When we got to the stop sign, I slipped out of line and headed south to Spoleto.

"Well, at least they know we recycle," offered Jill.

The only reason we were going to the supermarket and not some quaint village market was that we were looking for basics: toilet paper, garbage bags, dishwashing soap, vacuum cleaner bags, lightbulbs—moving-in kind of stuff. If there had been a Costco, that's where we would have headed. The supermarket in Spoleto is called the Coop—pronounced "kaawp"—and it's the only American-type establishment in Spoleto. It's big and bright and, at first glance, seems to be a replication of your standard Safeway or A&P.

At second glance, however, some major differences emerge. In the deli department, whole prosciuttos hang from the ceiling and the shelves display an endless array of salami, cooked hams, mortadella, pancetta and *guan-ciali*. These last two are what the Italians use for bacon—pancetta from the *pancia* or belly, *guanciali* from the cheek. In the re-frigerated dairy section, there are plastic containers of pancetta that has already been cubed—for the busy house-wife who's making carbonara in a hurry. There are two full aisles of olive oils—from cheap everyday stuff for sautéing to pricey extra-virgins that should be used only for "finish-ing" dishes ranging from salads to steaks. Along the back wall is a wine department with the best inventory and prices in town.

We filled our cart and got in line, trying to figure out the local customs for checking out. I noticed that you were ex-pected to bring your own sacks to carry your groceries home. If not, you had to purchase plastic bags at the check-out counter.

Across from us—in the next line over—was a young family with a cart nearly as full as ours. Their son—about five or six years old, I'd say—was clearly bored with the wait and had taken to bumping their shopping cart against everything he could find. When he finally rammed it into an elderly lady who was passing by, his father had had enough. He quickly and forcefully grabbed the boy by the shoulders and proceeded to read him the riot act. The boy stared at him, goggle-eyed. Then, without a moment's pause, the father bent down and kissed the boy tenderly on each cheek. We were definitely not in the A&P.

Max, who had taken in the whole scene, glanced over at me with a sly little smile on his face.

"How come you never did that to me, Pop?" he seemed to be saying. "How come you never kissed me on both cheeks after you yelled at me?"

Ten

ON SATURDAY, AFTER WE GOT THE BOYS off to the airport, I went to fill up my gas tank. I'd been putting it off and the tank was flashing urgent signs at me from the dashboard. I put it off because gas stations have never been easy for me in foreign countries. If it's self-serve, often as not I'll put in my credit card and never see it again. I don't know, either I push the wrong button or I put the card in upside down, but it's gone forever and I have to go through the whole nightmare of canceling everything and then trying to figure out exactly what my address is so they can send me another one. If it's full-serve I get even more anxious. I'll roll down the window and gesture to the tank and say, "*Pieno,*" which I know means "Fill it up" in Italian, and the attendant will start spewing an incomprehensible stream of language at me and then look expectantly for a reply. And I'll just shrug and say, "*Pieno*"—a little more forcefully this time. Then he'll smile and shake his head as if he's asking God for patience and walk away to serve somebody else. Once, in France, I put my credit card in the slot and, of

71

course, couldn't get it out and people behind me started honking and waving and the attendant came out and pointed to the gas pump and screamed, "Imbecile"—or its French equivalent—at me over and over. So I approach gas stations with a certain apprehension.

But this Saturday it went beautifully, I think because I'm getting a lot better with my Italian. The pay machine took my credit card smoothly, I pushed the number that corresponded to my pump, the card came back out and off I went to fill my tank, feeling rather fluent about the whole thing.

Then, on the way home, my car started bucking in third gear. You know that kind of surge-forward, lag-back pattern when you know your car isn't in the best of spirits? I dropped it to second and slowed down and the lurch went away, but I could feel that tightening of the steel band between my shoulder blades that I always get when I'm having a losing experience with a mechanical object.

Cheap gas, I thought. They probably watered it down.

I swung down into our little gravel road to pick up Jill; we were driving over the Umbrian border into Lazio to have dinner with some people we hadn't met yet—he's an Italian artist named Tonino who's close friends with an artist friend of ours and he and his family were very generous to Max when he was visiting Rome the week before. As we got down to the Flaminia and turned left, the car started in with its lurching thing again.

"Honey, I think I fucked up the car."

"What do you mean?"

"I think maybe I put the wrong gas in it."

"What gas did you use?"

"I put in unleaded but I'm getting a sneaking suspicion that this is a diesel."

"Can we get to Tonino's?"

"I'd be real nervous about getting on the highway like this."

It was over an hour's drive and I didn't want to get stuck on some dark, rural Italian highway.

"What about a gas station?"

As I said earlier, gas stations are not easy places for me. Even in America, speaking in my native tongue, I feel intimidated—no, shamed—when I have to reveal my utter ignorance about the machine I'm driving. And in this case, I'd have to admit to the gas station attendant that I had filled to the brim with unleaded gas (*sensa piomba*) the tank of a diesel car, which would surely evoke the most stringent looks of disdain; perhaps he would call all his Italian garage mechanic friends over to get a look at the schmuck who can't even figure out what kind of gas goes into his car. I tried to steer Jill away from that possibility.

"I think we better go home."

"Honey, they're expecting us!"

"Call them; I'm sure they'll understand. It's an emergency."

"Go to a gas station. I'm sure they can fix it."

By now, the car was lurching all the time. I stalled twice trying to steer it into the TAMOIL station, which was the biggest one on the Flaminia. I got into my "I'm just a stupid American" posture with my hands pressed in prayer in front of my chest and went up to the attendant.

"Uh . . . *scusi signori ma ce l'ho una problema. . . .*"

Sure enough, he started in with a machine-gun response from which I could pick up only the words "coffee" and "sofa"—I think. I started again. "*Il benzine*"—I pointed to the tank—"*errore . . . un sbaglio.*" Which means mistake. Then I danced around like an idiot indicating how stupid I was. He liked that. We were getting somewhere.

"*Che benzine?*" He pointed to the tank.

"*Senza piomba.*"

"*Quanti?*"

"*Pieno.*"

Sure enough, he started calling all his friends over, and I could fully understand his gestures as I watched him describe what I had done. They all laughed and shook their heads and, each in turn, told the story again, adding little twists and such. It would surely become a local legend.

Well, the upshot was that none of these grease-stained geniuses could fix it. It was Saturday, and the real mechanic didn't come in until Monday morning. They asked if I thought I could get the car home and I said, "*Speriamo,*" which means "Let's hope so" and is one of my best words. When I gave Jill the bad news, she somehow couldn't accept the fact that we weren't on our way to Lazio.

"Honey," she said, in not my favorite tone, "they're expecting us." A pause. "You never really wanted to go to their house for dinner, did you?"

Silently, I lurched the car off the Flaminia and headed toward home.

"What are we going to do?"

"We'll call them. They'll understand."

"I really was looking forward to wearing this new outfit tonight."

That, as far as I was concerned, was a complete non sequitur.

By a miracle, the car made it down our gravel road. We were safe. We would not be stranded out on some lonely Italian road, fighting off wolves through the dark, moonless night. I felt I had done my job—not without some resistance.

Once Jill changed out of her outfit, which had indeed been lovely, she seemed in a much better mood. She actually smiled at me.

"What'll we do for dinner?"

"We could walk up to Da Beppino," I offered.

We hadn't been there yet and it was actually just a short walk up the hill from our road. It had been recommended by Bruno as a place for big eaters; apparently, they did a legendary antipasto.

"Is this what you had in mind all along?"

"You mean did I put fifty dollars of the wrong gas into our rental car, probably wrecking it forever, just so that I could go to Da Beppino tonight?"

She smiled at me.

"Could be."

We hiked up the hill and entered the beautiful dining room, rustic but well-appointed, with good-looking waiters and waitresses scurrying busily around the room. We waited by the door until we caught the owner's eye.

"Uh . . . *non habbiamo una prenotazione, ma . . .*"

"*Due?*"

We nodded. Yes, we were two.

He led us to a lovely table in the center of the room.

"*Prendete gli antipasto sta sera?*"

Would we have the antipasto? Absolutely, we nodded with fervor. Because that's what this place is supposed to be all about.

That's all he needed to hear. He nodded to a waiter and off he went. We ordered our usual *acqua naturale*—no bubbles—and a carafe of red wine. In Umbria—especially out in the country—there was never any need to order fancy bottles. The local plonk was just fine.

After the water, the wine and the bread were on the table, a slow, sensuous dance began between the waitstaff and us. First, a lovely young lady came by with a delicious-smelling platter.

"*Cinghiale in pane?*"

We nodded and she gave us each a generous-sized piece of wild-boar sausage tucked inside a kind of brioche—steaming hot—and off she danced to another table. As we picked up our utensils to go to work on the sausage, another waiter appeared between us.

"*Risotto croquette?*"

We nodded and he placed one on each of our plates next to the sausage en croute. I didn't know where to look first.

"*Insalata di faro*"—a salad of spelt, tomato and arugula. Oh, yes.

"*Carpaccio daino?*"

We nodded again and accepted the deer carpaccio onto the center of our plates.

"*Prosciutto con tartuffi,*" another waiter announced, and onto the plate it came. This was the most exquisite house-made prosciutto, thinly sliced—or as they say over there, "*trasparente*" —wrapped around the most decadent paste of fresh, local black truffles. The salty-strong taste of the meat, cut against the funky-woodsy essence of the summer truffles, stopped us in our tracks. Well, almost.

"*Salami fata in casa.*" Exquisite thick-sliced salami—made downstairs.

"*Formaggio pecorino con miele di costagna*"—sharp, salty sheep's cheese drizzled with chestnut honey.

"*Carpaccio di oso.*" Goose carpaccio—superb.

"*Prosciutto in pane*"—this was a number. The waiter had rolled over a cart on which was a long, steaming brioche—like a Wellington, filled with fresh-cooked ham, which was coated with wild mushrooms and truffles. They use the same word—"prosciutto"—for preserved ham or cooked ham; the cooked is called *prosciutto cotto*. The waiter sliced off a very generous portion for each of us and managed to find room on our plates.

"*Pomodori gratinato*"—baked fresh tomatoes, drizzled with olive oil and bread crumbs.

"*Salsicce daino*"—deer sausage drizzled with long-aged *balsamica*.

We ate everything. We were in another dimension of eating.

The waiter came back to describe the pastas and Jill raised her arms in the international gesture of surrender. But I had a listen.

"*Ravioli con funghi porcini; strangozzi anche con porcini.*" I nodded, and soon large helpings of both were being heaped on my plate. Everything in Da Beppino is served family style. The pastas were wonderful. Porcini were just coming into season and the restaurant was very proud to have found the best of them.

Then our waiter came to the table and with only a hint of a smile, asked us what we'd like for dinner.

Later, we rolled down the hill to our cozy casa, happy to be home and safe, happy to be full and satisfied, smug that such a restaurant is a ten-minute walk from our place, and content—oh, so content—to be living this part of our life in Italy.

Sunday, not having the means to travel, we just hung around the house all day. We watered the garden, moved the furniture around in the living room and took a long walk through the olive groves. And I cooked three good meals from what was in the little fridge. It was our best day so far.

Monday morning I finally got through to the Avis people to tell them what I did to their car, and they handled it as if it were an everyday occurrence. They gave me the number for "*Assistenza*," which is like the AAA, who would come out and tow the car back to the rental office in Spoleto. They thought they would be able to drain the tank and get the car back to me by the afternoon.

Of course the *Assistenza* people spoke no English and, given the fact that our house has no address, I was having a hard time telling them where to come. So finally, in a flash of brilliance, I said, "Do you know Da Beppino?" I said this, of course, in impeccable Italian.

"Da Beppino—*il ristorante?*"

"*Si,*" said I.

The tow truck driver assured me he knew it very well.

"Let's meet there."

So I walked up the hill to the restaurant's driveway and leaned against their stone wall to wait for the tow truck—which was promised within a half hour, which I knew meant any time before lunch. After about five minutes, the two dogs that belong to the restaurant—perhaps the two best-fed dogs in the world—came sniffing down the driveway to see who was trespassing, and not far behind them came the owner who had fed us so well the night before.

"*É chiuso oggi,*" he called to me—like many restaurants in Italy, they close on Mondays.

I explained as best I could that I was waiting for the *Assistenza* and was using his place as a landmark. We then got into a very difficult conversation where I tried to explain what I had done to my car. His English was, if anything, worse than my Italian. When he finally got the picture—with the help of gestures and sounds—of my car bucking up the highway filled with the wrong gas, he beamed from ear to ear.

"Come, have a coffee."

When I protested and said that I'd better wait below for the tow truck, he waved and called over his shoulder that they would probably be hours.

"But it's your day of rest," I said.

He just waved and kept walking. He must have thought it was easier to make me a coffee than to try to have any more conversation.

We sat in the bar, had a few espressos and talked for the better part of the morning. And although I would swear that we didn't have more than five words in common, we got to know each other fairly well. I told him that I was an actor who wasn't working much anymore and about how my wife and I had bought the house down the hill, and he told me of all the show business people who have been to Da Beppino. And of a famous Italian director who planned a whole picture while staying in one of the rooms there, plowing through the famous antipasto every night. By the time the tow truck showed up, we were *vicini*—neighbors. And what better neighbor could you have if you want to go up the road to borrow a cup of goose carpaccio?

Eleven

"MARTIN'S A POOR, TORTURED little German boy," said JoJo with obvious affection. "He worries everything to death. But you won't find a better architect and he speaks perfect English—and given that I'll be supervising the whole project, I can whip him into shape when he starts losing sleep over the color of your septic tank or some such nonsense."

She was holding forth under the pergola while Jill and I were picking over the remains of breakfast—prosciutto, melon, yogurt, toasted unsalted Umbrian bread with chestnut-honey and coffee. JoJo was gearing up to negotiate the deal for our *amplificazione*—the addition of two more bedrooms onto the Rustico. One of the real perks when we bought the house was our set of approved plans for doubling its size—"approved" being the operative word, in that it's virtually impossible to get permission to build in the olive groves unless there's an intact structure already there. And even then, permission to improve it or alter it can take years of frustrating negotiations with the *comune*. JoJo has played this role with many of her real estate clients, serving as a go-between, translator and general gadfly so that their planning and building process doesn't get mired in transcontinental misunderstandings. Just as when she was in the agent business, she protects her clients like a mother lion. She is the agent Jill and I have always dreamed of having—loyal, attentive and fierce. And always amusing.

"I usually work with Maurizio, who's also a good architect. But his English sucks and you guys can't speak enough Italian yet. You'd end up building something you don't want."

"You've never worked with Martin?" Jill asked.

"No, we've never tried it. He and Karen are good friends of ours and we cook dinners for each other all the time, but I think he's afraid of me. I can be a little outspoken."

This was a monumental understatement. I told her we were thinking of putting the whole thing off for a year or two, of just enjoying the place we bought and worrying about construction somewhere down the line.

"It's kind of a plus not to be able to have any guests," I said.

"No argument there," said JoJo. "But be careful. Restrictions around here are getting tighter, not looser. They don't want this area to become another Tuscany, with little English Tudor tea shops all over the place. In a couple of years, you may well have lost your window of opportunity to build—permit or no."

Martin's car had pulled up at the gate and I went inside and pushed the electric gate opener to let him in. As he parked and got out of his car, we could see he was carrying a sheaf of rolled-up architectural plans. I offered him some coffee.

Jojo

"No, thank you. I've had my quota of caffeine already this morning. Good morning, JoJo; have you been telling them what a wonderful architect I am?"

Martin is an elegantly handsome man. With his blond hair, steel-blue eyes and pink cheeks, he is the very model of a modern major Aryan. His clothes—even at his most casual—hang on him perfectly.

"Oh sure," answered JoJo. "I've been singing your praises."

They smiled at each other. Then Martin turned to us.

"To build in Italy, it's a very good idea to have a German architect. This way, things will get done on time and on budget."

Martin blushed, acknowledging the German stereotype. We all nodded, realizing it was probably quite true.

"I have here three things to show you. First, Bruno's original plans—just to get an idea of what he had in mind. . . ."

"They don't want to do Bruno's plans. They want two bedrooms."

"Please, JoJo, let me make my presentation and then—when I have finished—you can give your opinion. Which I'm sure you won't be shy about."

"Quite right."

They smiled at each other again.

"Then I have a drawing for an addition with two master bedrooms, each with a bathroom en suite."

He paused and glared significantly at JoJo.

"And then I have another plan that would completely redefine the house—just to show you that anything is possible here."

"They don't want to redefine the house. They love it. That's why they bought it. Why the hell would they want to knock it down and start over?"

"I'm not suggesting knocking anything down, JoJo. My God! What do you think I am? I have worked harder to preserve the integrity and history of these Umbrian farmhouses than any Italian architect you can name!"

Martin was getting a little red under the collar, and we could see that JoJo was enjoying every minute of it.

"Good. So we're not knocking it down; we're all agreed on that."

"But I think—if JoJo will allow me to have a consultation with my clients—that you should open your minds to the possibilities."

We nodded. It didn't seem like such a bad idea to us. Martin unrolled a drawing on the table.

"In this scenario, I have the kitchen in the new part of the house. That way you can design your dream kitchen from the ground up."

"I'm pretty happy with the kitchen, actually . . . ," I said, nervously. "I don't want to get into a million-dollar restoration here."

"Exactly!" piped up JoJo. "Bruno wasn't going to spend any more than a hundred fifty thousand euro on the whole thing."

"Bruno was doing a completely different plan! My God! Bruno wanted only one bedroom!"

Martin was now turning bright red.

"Correct me if I'm wrong," JoJo said to us. "You guys want to add two bedrooms, you want to keep it simple, you want to match the stonework so it looks like the old Rustico—and not have all that tortured rusted metal and glass that Martin likes to put on things."

"If you're talking about the house I did in Trevi, you know very well that you love that house. It's why you recommended me here today."

"True, that's a great house. I just love making your ears red."

Then she turned to us.

"Why don't you go and see some of Martin's work—the traditional houses and some of the tortured ones as well. Then you can make up your own minds."

"Let's make it for next week," said Jill. "Caroline's arriving this coming Sunday and she'll want to be in on the process."

We all readily agreed to this. Martin took out his appointment book and we set up an afternoon the following Tuesday for a house tour and lunch that sounded like a lot of fun. Martin was growing on me by the minute. He clearly had a lot of pride in his work.

"Who are you thinking of to build it?" JoJo asked him.

"I've been working with Fidelio and I think finally I know how to handle his little quirks."

"I won't work with him," she said flatly.

"I can handle him, JoJo."

"He's a thief and I'm not gonna work with him."

Then Martin started to explain to us that JoJo and this Fidelio had gotten into quite a shouting match over a project they were doing together the year before. It had become a much-talked-about local incident.

"He is from the south, and they're not used to hearing a woman talk like that," said Martin.

"You mean like when I told him to shove his bill up his Neapolitan ass?"

"Yes, that and other things. Worse things."

"Well, I won't work with him." She turned to us. "Ask Bruno. He'll tell you what a crook he is."

"Bruno does not know everything, JoJo."

"Find another contractor."

Martin

After a pause, Martin suggested that he and JoJo work this out between themselves and that we, as clients, needn't worry ourselves with these details. Behind his eyes, however, I could see that he was thinking forward to at least a year of being second-guessed by JoJo and wondering whether it was worth it. As much as I liked Martin and felt I could trust him, I wasn't ready to lose JoJo on the project. She would be our agent, our staunch advocate when we were six thousand miles away. And she would watch the purse strings. No, they'd just have to learn to get along.

"Could I ask a technical question?" asked Jill, changing the subject.

"Of course. You're the client," said Martin, beaming.

"What do we do for electrical sockets? I can't find more than one plug in the living room."

"You do what any good owner of a three-hundred-and-fifty-year-old house does—you buy an extension cord."

JoJo piped up to say that she knew where we could get one and suggested we follow her into Spoleto. Then, she said, we could grab a little lunch up at the Piazza Mercato.

"I will leave you to it. Some of us, unfortunately, must work for a living," said Martin as he gathered his plans and bid us good-bye.

The electric shop in Spoleto was small, featuring shelves piled high with lamps, toasters, fans and TVs—all in various states of repair. There was one man behind the counter and two people in front of us in line. While we were waiting, JoJo filled us in a bit more about Martin. She said he had an excellent reputation—not only for his work, but for his ability to deal with the local bureaucracies that hand out building permits in each *comune,* or township. Our area, she told us, is one of the most difficult areas to get permission to build—because of the olive groves, which are fiercely protected from development. She then confided that if it hadn't been for Martin's abilities to persuade, pester and cajole the authorities, our permit—which had already been approved—could have taken a year or two to actually be delivered into our hands. Now, she said, we would need his talents even more to get them to quickly approve our *variazione*—meaning the changes from Bruno's approved plans to our altered ones. The footprint, the square footage and the pool design would have to be exactly the same, and whatever changes we did inside would need the approval of the *comune.*

Eventually, our turn came to speak to the man behind the counter of the electric store. JoJo let us try to handle it ourselves. I had already looked up the word for extension cord before we left the house, so I was feeling confident. I noticed there were three people in line behind us, but I figured we wouldn't be but a moment. Just an extension cord, after all.

"*Buon giorno, signore,*" I started. "*Ho bisogno una prolunga.*"

"Ah!" he said. "*Perche?*"

He wanted to know what we wanted to use it for. Jill and I then got into a discussion about what our particular needs were—portable tape player, two lamps, a laptop computer and a TV, with only one electrical outlet on that side of the living room. As we explained the layout of the room, he took out a pen and paper and had us draw it for him. Then we negotiated the perfect length for the cord and the right number of plugs for the end. That led us to a discussion of color. I looked nervously behind me at the line, which had gotten longer; but no one seemed to be in a hurry. The line had transmogrified into a discussion group and they were all talking quite happily about God only knows what. After a long discussion of our own, we decided on *marrone*—brown.

Then he carefully measured out the length of cord, cut it and set about to connect the plugs on either end. He worked slowly and meticulously, as if he were creating a fine work of art. By the time he was done, we thought so, too. It was, without a doubt, the finest extension cord I have ever owned.

He then wrapped it up in brown paper, put a rubber band around it and proudly handed it to me.

"*Quanto costa?*" I asked.

It was a dollar and change. For a masterpiece.

Twelve

ON SUNDAY, JILL AND I DROVE DOWN TO THE ROME airport to pick up Caroline, who had finally arrived to stake a claim on her share of the Rustico. When she emerged from customs with an exhausted frown on her face, Jill reached into her purse—which seems to hold all the world's goods—and produced a mortadella sandwich. Once we managed to get a few bites of it into our tired, frazzled Korean, she perked up considerably; some people are easy. As we walked to the parking lot, Caroline filled us in about the triathlon she had triumphantly completed the day before. She had to swim a full mile across an ice-cold lake, peel off her wet suit and immediately jump on a bike and pedal twenty-six miles—up and down steep hills—then ditch the bike and proceed to grind out a six- mile run to the finish line. Then, with barely a day to recuperate, she'd hopped on a plane and flown fourteen hours to Rome.

"I slept the whole way—like a rock. Right through all the airplane food!"

I told her that we had an invitation that night to go with

Bruce and JoJo to a *sagra,* which is kind of a harvest festival, but we'd completely understand if she wanted to pass on it.

"No, I have to eat dinner, after all," she said, chewing happily on the sandwich. "But I'll see how I feel later; maybe I'll crash from the jet lag."

We pulled out of the airport parking lot and Jill and Caroline immediately fell into conversation, catching each other up on all kinds of things. I focused on the driving and let my mind wander, the soothing, burbling white noise of their girl talk easing me into a blissful meditative state.

The drive up from Rome is just under two hours and it works as a kind of decompression chamber. Once you clear the Grand Raccordo Annulare, the ring road that circles the Eternally Chaotic City, the noise, the traffic, the fumes, the impatient honking, the road rage all slip away behind you as the scenery shifts from urban sprawl to farms, haystacks and little ancient hill towns in the distance looking down on the strip of highway that cuts through on its way to Florence and beyond. We exit the A1 at a little town called Orte and headed east into Umbria. When we clear Terni, the highway narrows into a two-lane country road—the Via Flaminia— which heads north through a steep valley into Spoleto. Just south of town, we pass by a sign on the side of the road for a local bar called the Bar Belli. Both Jill and Caroline get a big kick out of observing that it must have been named after me. I press down a little harder on the accelerator whenever we get to that point in the road, hoping to slip by it unnoticed, but so far, no luck. The Bar Belli. Very amusing.

A few minutes later—once the hilarity had cooled down—we passed beneath the breathtaking aqueduct that spans the deep gorge between the town and the mountain on the other side and we knew we were home.

After Caroline unpacked and reacquainted herself with the house, the three of us took a long hike up the hill to the Castello and beyond. We walked on a path through the woods that twists up and around, finally emerging at Silvignano, the little *borgo* that sits on the hill overlooking our property. A *borgo* is a loose collection of houses—always without shops, cafés or restaurants, but still big enough to get a name of its own. The houses of Silvignano are the only neighbors we can see from the Rustico. When we got back down the hill, Caroline decided to take a *pisolino*—that's a little nap—so that she'd be up for going to the *sagra* that night.

Bruce and JoJo picked us up around seven o'clock and we drove about forty-five minutes to a little town called Canarra, which is in the farm country just south of Assisi. Canarra also happens to be where St. Francis did his famous talk with the birds. Along the way, Bruce filled us in on what we were about to experience.

"There are *sagras* all over Italy. For most towns, the *sagra* is the sole source of revenue for the entire year. It'll help to pay for equipping the fire department or erecting a war memorial in the piazza . . . whatever. And the whole town pitches in."

"The best is the goose *sagra* in Bettona," chipped in JoJo. "Goose done every way you can imagine—and some ways you can't."

"What about the snail *sagra* in the Valnerina?"

"Garden pests. I can't stomach them. I don't know what you see in them, to tell you the truth."

"Even a snail needs love, Joanna."

"You don't love them; you eat them."

Bruce smiled his little Cheshire cat grin. He's been playing straight man to JoJo for years, and they have their act down pat.

"What about the one at Lago Bolsena?" said JoJo. "That's probably the best, if you had to choose."

"They hold it every year on Ash Wednesday. Most *sagras* are in the summer—when the crops are coming in—but Lago Bolsena's is in the middle of the winter."

"Ash Wednesday—rain or shine."

"They cook everything in these giant cauldrons—fish from the lake—and the cooks wear asbestos suits to avoid getting incinerated."

"And you have to bring your own plate, your own silverware, everything."

"Yeah. All they provide is the fish."

"It's a madhouse. You have to reserve months in advance."

We couldn't get any closer to Canarra than a half-mile away. We parked alongside the road and hiked in with hundreds of other people. Canarra's is an onion *sagra*. Their onions are famously sweet—much like Mauis or Vidalias—and when the crop comes in, you can find them featured all over Italy.

The tiny town was packed with people. All the stores were open and set up like booths at a carnival. And in the four main piazzas, giant tents had been constructed to serve as restaurants. There were long lines at every one, but the turnover was pretty fast. The cooks were recruited from the men and women of the town—Canarrians, I suppose—who had been cooking these recipes for generations. Once we got inside, we found seats at one of the long tables—everything was family style—and in no time, a young woman came up to take our order. She was clearly not a professional. She shouted at us over the din to hurry up and order; we shouted back what we wanted. We ordered onion soup—served with onion bread; then pasta with bacon and onions, which was a knockout; then various meat dishes—smothered with onions, of course; then a big plate of fried onions for the middle of the table. There was an onion and fennel salad—to cleanse the palate—and we finished up with onion ice cream, which was as bad as it sounds. We washed all this down with pitchers of young red wine.

After we paid up—making our contribution to the local economy—we walked through the little streets, burping merrily along with the rest of the crowd. There were stands selling all sorts of products—onion compotes, strings of fresh onions, onion artifacts of all kinds. And there was one piazza set up for dancing, with a live band and colored lights strung from building to building. Everyone danced exactly the same—a kind of fox trot, I think. It was as if they had all studied at the same Arthur Murray's.

Caroline bought a chance at a stand called the Fish Pond. She reached into a bowl that was held high above her head by an elderly woman with very few teeth, in a black dress. She unfolded the paper and handed it the woman, who looked at it for a long time with a serious look on her face. Then that woman showed it to another woman in black and then to a third. They huddled and started talking excitedly, pointing to Caroline, who—being the only Asian person for hundreds of miles—stuck out in the crowd anyway.

"*Il pesce! Il pesce!*"

Caroline, it seems, had won the grand prize—the *pesce*. The fish. The prize, however, was not a fish, but a prosciutto—a whole prosciutto that they proceeded to take down from where it was hanging and give to Caroline. She was dazed—not only from jet lag, but from all these women in black dresses screaming at her in Italian.

Caroline's Prosciutto

They insisted that she march through the streets, holding the prosciutto for all to see. Bruce explained that they wanted everyone to know that it was actually possible to win something at their booth. Caroline cradled the ham in her arms like a baby, and we all pointed at it and screamed, "*Il pesce!*" until everyone understood that she had won the grand prize.

"Bruce can show you how to slice it properly. It's an art," said JoJo, once we had schlepped the heavy ham the half-mile to the car.

"Well, you need a prosciutto holder. You can't do anything without that. Then a very sharp knife and you're in business. After three or four years' practice, of course."

We drove home over the twisting, dark roads, digesting our onions, listening to Bruce cheerfully holding forth on the fine art of prosciutto slicing.

Thirteen

IT SEEMS WE NEVER HAD TIME TO GET THINGS DONE because our days were filled to the brim with lingering. Breakfast became a longer and longer linger. Not mine, which is just coffee and a crossword puzzle. But Jill and Caroline have a way of making breakfast into a full-length play which unfolds in long, slow, Chekhovian acts—from the yogurt and peaches, into the cheese, prosciutto, tomatoes and *panini,* into the biscotti dipped in chestnut honey, all washed down with tea. By the time they're done with that, it's time to get ready to meet JoJo at the hardware store, where we'll spend ten minutes buying a screwdriver and then all go off to a three-hour lunch, feeling like we'd had a very productive morning. And if we're planning on having any dinner at all, forget it; that's the day.

But one morning we got focused. We had a little breakfast meeting and decided we had to do something about the language problem—*la problema con la lingua.*

We were coming along too slowly, we decided. We had studied in California before we left, which helped Jill and I remember some of what we had learned twenty-five years earlier. And Caroline was fluent in French and German, which helped her *understand* people much better than we could, but she couldn't actually *speak* much Italian. And she refused to study with us because she thought we were further along and she didn't want to feel left behind. I felt I was the strongest at this point, almost fluent in restaurants—as long as no one spoke back to me. In short, we needed work.

We got a recommendation from Bruce, who is in the language business, about a fellow he knows in Spoleto who is supposed to be very good, and we called him and left a message. But since we still can't read the instructions for our Italian answering machine, we never did get in touch with him.

Then Karen, Martin's wife, told us about another teacher whom she thought we would love. Her name is Paola, she's local and she's married to an Australian architect named Ken. We called her and booked our first class. Caroline, of course, demurred. She mumbled something about having to learn in her own way and disappeared the moment Paola's car came up the driveway.

Unlike other Italian teachers, Paola was mostly interested in showing off her English, which she insisted she spoke without accent.

"Today"—which rhymes with "g'day" from the Aussie beer commercials—"we will larn to spik alla de words for when first you grit each other."

And we were off. Eventually, we got her to speak in Italian, which she does beautifully though with, admittedly, a regional quirk—a "sh" for "s" that gives her speech a kind of marbles-in-the-dust sound, each word rolling easily into and over the next, connected by little swishy sounds. Not at all unpleasant.

Each class had a theme. One day, we'd talk about the garden and learn all that vocabulary; another, we'd talk about our families and where we grew up. It was all conversation, and we were starting to get into the rhythm of it, but Caroline always stayed hidden upstairs, secretly listening through the window. Until the day the mortadella came up.

I think I brought it up first because we had bought some gorgeous mortadella in a pork store in Norcia the day before and I brought it out to show Paola, and as she started to hold forth on the glories of Italian cured meats, Caroline burst through the kitchen door.

"*Buon giorno, Paola, come stai?*"

The power of deli.

"Don't ever buy in Norcia," lectured Paola to the three of us. "Norcia is a rip-off."

It sounded like "reepov."

"Even for Italians. If you don't have the local accent, you will pay *doppio* [double]."

"But they have good mortadella," I put in.

"Who can eat when you pay so much?" We were learning that Paola can be very, very bossy when it comes to food.

"I will take you to find the best mortadella."

"When?"

"We will shop together. It will be a lesson. And then we will cook together."

"*Scusi, Paola. . . .*" Caroline, suddenly fluent.

"*Dové il mortadella migliore?*" She was asking which store had the best cold cuts.

"The best—*il migliore*—is from my childhood."

The three of us sat down quietly under the pergola and gave her the stage.

"In the morning, before I go to school, my mama

would go to the local *fornaio* (baker) to buy the *pane cotto a legna*."

This is the local unsalted bread freshly baked in the traditional wood oven.

"You can buy *un kilo*"—she shows with her hands—"or *un mezzo kilo*"—she shows half as much.

"She would buy the mortadella—*trasparente* [very thinly sliced]—and put it between the slices of bread, which were still warm from the oven. Then she would wrap it tightly in paper and I would take it to school. Then at eleven o'clock—the hour of the *recesso*—all the children would take their *panini* out of the paper and by then, the mortadella and the bread had grown together into each other, and the taste. . . ."

She shook her head from side to side in a reverie; her cheeks were pink and her eyes brimmed with tears as she remembered this moment of childhood bliss.

"A little butter on the bread?" I whispered.

"*Burro,* NO!" Suddenly the soft moment vanished; her eyes were steely blue.

"*Burro,* NO!" Again. If anything, stronger, hinting violence.

"So no butt—"

"*NIENTE. Pane,* cooked in the wood; mortadella, sliced *trasparente. Basta cosi.* You Americans have always to add things. Mayonnaise—to cover up the taste of your bad meat."

So, no butter.

Two days later, we went shopping with a plan to cook together that evening. We'd have Ken, Paola's husband, and Jane and Freddy, our English friends that we met in Puglia at the McAlpines. We picked Paola up at the Fonti di Clitunno down on the Flaminia at around ten and all started off to Spoleto. The first stop was the *feramente* (hardware store) where we bought a *girarosto,* a gizmo that you set up in your fireplace to cook chickens on a turning spit. Something no Italian home should be without. We also picked up some other essentials, like a sign that said "Beware of the dog" in Italian which we would take back to the States. Then, we were off to the *macelleria*—Paola's favorite in Spoleto—to get meat for dinner.

The butcher shop is on the road that leads down to the railway station in Spoleto. It's spotlessly clean, has no sign of any kind outside and is, like everything else that's good in Italy, a family operation. Lauro, owner, father, husband, butcher *straordinario,* runs the show—flirting and teasing with the customers, strict and precise with his wife and daughters, who fill the orders and ring up the sales. He's a big presence. But Paola is ready for him.

"*Un pollo, pulito.*" A chicken, cleaned. That means head, neck, feet and feathers removed. Lauro disappears into the back for a moment and returns with a beautiful chicken— about three and a half pounds, to my eye—with most but not all of the feathers removed.

"*Anche il cuore, il fegato, e lardo.*" Paola requests the heart and the liver of our bird along with a healthy portion of *lardo,* which is . . . well, *lardo.* But not the soaplike, hydrogenated, supermarket lard we have in the States; this is pristine, white, fresh pork fat from under the ribs of Umbrian pigs, the best in the world. He gave us what looked like a bit more than a quarter pound.

"From these we will make our *battuto,*" says Paola. "We chop very finely the heart, the liver, the *lardo* along with *una testa di alio*"—a head of garlic.

"*E un po di rosmarino,*" adds Lauro.

"*Si, certo, rosmarino. Anche sale, anche pepe,*"

Rosemary; also salt; also pepper.

"So we chop all this up together, right? A whole head of garlic?"

"What means, 'head'?"

"That means the whole garlic." I show her with my hand.

"NO! *TROPPO!* Only one little head." She shows me with her thumb and forefinger.

Okay; clove.

"We chop together and . . . *come si dice?*" Paola makes a violent gesture with her fist.

"Pound?"

"*Si,* pound. Until it is a very nice paste. This we will rub inside and outside our *pollo.*"

Then we asked Lauro for some *costine di maiale*—pork ribs—cut into two-rib sections that we would grill over the fireplace while our chicken was resting after its rotisserie spin. Paola and Lauro insisted that the ribs should take no more than ten to fifteen minutes over the hot coals.

Then we bought some thick-cut strips of pancetta— about six or seven of them, to be diced for the pasta. That was it for dinner, but Caroline wanted some mortadella, which Lauro sliced *trasparente* according to Paola's instructions. Then he showed us some of his house-made *coralina,* which is like salami, but better. We got a half pound of that (250 *grammi*).

Caroline now had that gleam in her eye that signals a major shopping binge, and Jill was trying to gently pull her out the door when Lauro started carving thick slices from a whole roast pork that he had stashed below the counter.

"*Assaggiate un pocchino.*" Taste this.

We tried to indicate that we didn't really need any more

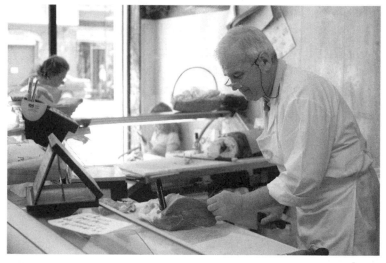

Lauro

lunch meat, but Lauro, as I said, is a very powerful presence. We tasted. And it was stunning. The pork literally melted in our mouths. Not poetically; it actually melted. Perfectly seasoned, delicately roasted, remarkably fresh—that's the real secret—it transcended any previously held concept I had about pig.

We wrenched Caroline away from the *macelleria* and headed back north to Campello, where we'd do the rest of the shopping—salad, onion, garlic, pasta and wine. I thought we'd do that with Paola and then I'd drop her back at her car. But when I turned on the Flaminia toward the *alimentari,* she commanded from the backseat,

"Mike [also rhymes with "g'day"], STOP!"

She said this with such a sense of urgency that I felt I had to do something immediately—even though I was on a highway, with large trucks coming in both directions.

"STOP, MIKE!"

I managed a left turn between the oncoming trucks, into a small parking lot and turned to the backseat to deal with what I was sure was a severe medical emergency.

"I have to get home to cook lunch for Ken. It's almost one o'clock."

Paola came over to the house around five-thirty to help us with the prep for the feast. I had already made the *battuto,* chopping, then pounding, the innards, the *lardo,* the garlic and rosemary, the salt and pepper into a paste. We had also put the ribs into a bath of olive oil, garlic, rosemary, salt and pepper (sound familiar?). Then Paola instructed Caroline, who had never before had her hand inside a chicken, to take charge of the bird.

"First, we wash in *vino bianco*—inside and out. Then dry very carefully. Then we take the *battuto* and rub it into the skin of the chicken; also inside—all over."

Caroline closed her eyes, scrunched up her face and dipped her hand into the larded chicken guts while Jill stood by with a camera, documenting the insertion. After the chicken was coated with the *battuto,* Paola instructed Caroline to poke four holes into the bird's meatiest parts and, using a rosemary twig, to push the *battuto* down into the holes, leaving the rosemary sticking out. Then Jill, who sews, stepped in to truss the chicken so that it didn't flop around on the rotisserie.

Meanwhile, I was building a good fire in our fireplace, which, like any good Italian *camino,* is built for cooking— plenty of space on either side of the fire so that when something's finished you can rest it there to keep it warm. It's also equipped with a grill with an adjustable rack—which we'd use later for the ribs.

Paola called to me from the kitchen to plunge the iron spit into the hottest part of the fire to make sure it was free of any contamination. Then, when it cooled a bit, we speared the chicken, secured it on the *girarrosto* and got it turning in front of the flames. Two hours. Basted with rosemary sprigs dipped in oil.

Now it was time to marinate the cooks. We opened a bottle of Montefalco Rosso, the first of many to flow that night. Montefalco is a hill town a few miles north of us on the Flaminia and is the wine capital of the central part of Umbria. Their most famous wine is Montefalco Sangrantino, which can easily command fifty bucks a bottle back home, but the Rosso, which is a blend, less sophisticated and costs around eight euros a bottle, was more than fine. We toasted to new friends, to fresh starts—and to our chicken, which was slowly releasing its mélange of aromas as it browned over the coals.

The pasta for the evening was a version of spaghetti carbonara—made without the usual eggs, so it was less heavy, more fitting for a late summer evening. Caroline put the water on to boil and cut the strips of pancetta into a quarter-inch dice—the smaller the better. Then she finely diced one small onion and a clove—not a head—of garlic and grated a hefty mound of *parmigiano*. She would wait until the last minute to finish it.

Freddy and Jane, our English buddies, arrived with more bottles of wine for the feast. They had spent the day in Perugia and were filled with stories of what they'd seen. Jane's in public relations and Freddy's a sportswriter who covers boxing matches for a London newspaper. Their dry

Jane, Caroline, Paola, and Jill in the kitchen

English wit is an asset to any dinner party. Then Ken, Paola's husband, pulled up and we were under way. Ken is as diffident as Paola is exuberant—a perfect match. But he loosened up considerably with the wine and was soon regaling us, in his distinctive Melbourne accent, with stories of how they met and courted.

Jill and Jane took charge of the setting of the table which, with seven people around it, filled our little kitchen to the limit. Caroline and Paola finished making the salad and the dressing. And the men kept company with the chicken in the other room. When we all agreed it was done perfectly, we put it to rest on a platter and placed the ribs on the grill over the coals.

At that point, Caroline put the spaghetti into the salted

water and started the carbonara. Under Paola's direction, she poured quite a bit more olive oil into the pan than any cookbook has ever authorized—covering the bottom to a depth of a quarter inch. When this got hot, in went the diced onion, then the garlic, then the pancetta—almost a pound of it, finely diced. She browned this all together and stirred the spaghetti, tasting it to see when it was done. When the pasta was just a chew short of al dente she drained it and finished it in the hot oil and bacon. Then the grated *parmigiano* was incorporated; and then a healthy grind or three of fresh pepper over the top—which is, by the way, how carbonara got its name—and it was on the table.

I finished the ribs, cut up the chicken and put all the meat on a platter by the fire to warm for our *secondi*. Then I sat down to join the merry throng around the table, inhaling the carbonara, the wine, the aroma of the meats, the brew of accents and languages that flew around the table and the laughter that somehow made them all comprehensible.

Fourteen

THERE'S A STRING—probably a monofilament of some kind because it can't be seen by the human eye; yet it's durable enough to maintain its strength for a lifetime, and it's long enough to reach across oceans. One end connects to the most delicate and vulnerable part of my reproductive organs and the other end rests comfortably in Jill's hand. And whenever she feels the need, she gives it a smart little tug and gets me to do whatever she wants.

The issue, it seems, was that I had been accelerating my food and wine intake from the day we arrived in Umbria and Jill felt it was her job to hose me down somehow. The food was so seductive, the wines so drinkable, the grappa so stimulating, that any sense of moderation—not a big word in my vocabulary anyway—had vanished into an ever-spreading fog of indulgence. Long lunches—always with a bottle or two of wine—flowed into even longer dinners that ended with a seemingly bottomless jug of grappa. The amazing thing about grappa is that the first whiff of it is quite off-putting. It starts out tasting not unlike a cheap brand of lighter fluid. But with each succeeding sip the taste improves, until, by the fourth or fifth glass, it's like mother's milk to me.

Often mornings were tinged with regret and remorse, but my memory of pleasure far outweighed the fleeting moments of pain, and I was usually my old, indulgent self by the time I finished my second cup of coffee. And by lunchtime I was up and ready to get the old ball rolling again. Shall it be Fontanelle, with its grilled meats brought to the table on your very own portable hibachi? Or Il Pescatore, with its shellfish antipasto of the freshest clams, oysters, mussels, cockles and whelks—some raw, some delicately poached in an herb-scented seafood broth? Fontanelle would be red wine, of course—to go with the meat; and perhaps an Orvieto Classico would slide down perfectly with the seafood at Pescatore. Or should we drive up the mountain to Pettino for the pasta with wild boar sauce?

And then I felt the little tug. Well, not so little, actually. It came in the form of a seemingly innocent inquiry one day after breakfast.

"Do you need the car this morning?" asked Jill.

"No. Why? Where are you going?"

"To the gym."

"The . . . ?"

"The gym. Want to go?"

An icy claw gripped my spine. I faintly remembered hearing this word before. It had a bad connotation, a sinister ring.

"Jimm?" I struggled to place it. "Jimm?" Surely not an Italian word.

"It'll be good. Get your blood flowing again."

Caroline had put this idea in her head, I'm sure. Caroline, who was off—as she was every morning—riding hundreds of miles up and down hills on her bicycle, staying in top triathlon shape. She tacitly shamed Jill, and now Jill was trying to pass the guilt on to me.

I had no idea there was such a thing as a gym in Italy. It's not really in the Italian character, which was one of the reasons I wanted to emigrate. But apparently Martin and Karen had told Jill about a place up the road from us toward Trevi that had the requisite treadmills, StairMasters and other medieval instruments of torture that make up a gym. "*Palestra*" is the Italian word. I was surprised to hear that they actually had a term for it. There is, for example, no word in the Italian language for hangover.

Jill changed into her exercise outfit, laced up her sneakers and kissed me good-bye.

"I'll see you in an hour or so." And off she went.

This is the way she works: small, intermittent injections of guilt that slowly work their way into my system to undermine my resolve. But I have fought these battles before and—tug on my testicles or no—I wasn't going down without a fight. This was another of her insidious plots to undermine my fun—like her pasta-only-once-a-day campaign. Can you imagine?

I watched the car bump up the dirt road and turn south toward the Flaminia, and then ran into the kitchen and put on another pot of coffee. Ha! Take that. I would flood my system with caffeine. There's more than one way to get the blood moving.

When she came back, she was all rosy and buff, flaunting her endorphins, trying to make me feel inferior and fat. But I didn't bite. I just said I was glad she had a good time. She smiled. I smiled.

No blood—a Mexican standoff.

After a few futile days of trying to shame me into the gym, she stepped up the game with a two-pronged attack— the old carrot-and-stick routine. On the one hand she implied that our sex life would be better if I worked out, on the other that I would die of a massive heart attack if I didn't. She was closing in for the kill, and I decided I'd better go on the offensive before all was lost.

"This is your problem, honey, not mine," I told her. "You're going to the gym out of guilt. Life in Italy is just too pleasurable for you and you feel you have to inject some pain into it."

"Excuse me?"

"It's a gentile thing—that Calvinist, Lutheran crap you guys have foisted on the world. Let's all dedicate ourselves to pain and suffering and if God forbid a little pleasure, a little indulgent fun comes our way, we'll run and hide and pray that the devil won't get us."

"Are you saying I don't like pleasure?"

I shrugged.

"Didn't I just tell you how good it makes me feel? Is it possible there are other kinds of pleasure than just cramming food and drink down your gullet?"

I decided to stay mute and mope for a while. This can be a very effective form of argument—especially when you have nothing intelligent to say.

Then she went really low—she said she was being serious. Up to this point I'd been enjoying our little fencing match, but now she wanted to get real, to get actual.

"You'll feel better, baby. And you'll live longer." And a little moisture started to well up in the corners of her beautiful baby blues.

"Aw," I whined. "Don't do that."

"Just try it. For me."

Jesus Christ.

The next day, like a condemned man, I donned my traditional workout uniform that I had worn to the gym in Mill Valley—khaki pants, a golf shirt and an old cashmere sweater with the sleeves rolled up. Going to a gym in California is somehow different. It's a law. Everyone in California is fit and toned and healthy and bronzed, and if you don't buy into that you can get in trouble with the authorities. If

Jill in the orto

you're pasty and fat in California, they take away your driver's license.

But Italy's a whole other kind of civilization, an older, wiser culture where the dogged pursuit of perspiration is not mankind's highest goal. It's a philosophical country. One sits at table—yes, there may be a bit of food and drink at hand—and one discourses with colleagues on the many thorny questions of life. Like, perhaps, what one is going to eat at one's next meal, which will be coming up in a few hours.

Like most other businesses in Umbria, the *palestra* in Trevi is a family operation. Marco and his wife, Paola, are the proprietors—both cut like bodybuilders, their faces flashing that expression that says they know they're healthier and more disciplined than you. Their daughter could be seen sitting in the office doing her homework and practicing her smug expression so that one day she could take over.

Jill introduced me to everybody and right away Marco asked me if I wanted to buy a ten-day pass which, he urged, could save me a lot of money in the long run. I tried to explain that I wasn't interested in the long run, that I liked to live for the moment, but Jill jumped right in with the credit card. I felt like my idyllic life in Italy was being hijacked right before my eyes.

In the corner was a spin class in full operation. The teacher, Daniele, was another ridiculously toned guy in a tank top, pedaling away and calling out instructions to his adoring class of housewives.

"*Salire!*" he boomed out, and they all shifted their gears to start the climb. Then he got off his bike and walked around giving intimate, individual instructions to the women, who, I must say, were not minding his attention one bit. I'm sure this kind of flirting takes place in American gyms, but it all seemed so much more obvious in Italy.

Jill drifted over to an elliptical trainer, a seriously dangerous-looking contraption, and I got myself going on a treadmill that was parked in front of the TV. If there's anything more painful than physical exercise, it's Italian TV. Especially daytime TV. As my thighs slowly roused themselves from their weeks of lethargy, I watched a woman, made up like a cheap hooker, constantly bending over for no other reason than to flaunt her rather extraordinary breasts to the camera. It seems she had to choose between three loutish young men to see which one would get to go behind the curtain and have his way with her during the commercial break. She questioned each one in turn, asking them to imagine themselves in situations that were dripping with sexual innuendo, and they outdid one another, leering and preening like peacocks and all but exposing themselves, each trying to prove that he was the most sexually desirable man in the world. Fortunately, I couldn't understand anything.

Except that I was in pain. I understood that. My legs felt like they were moving through mud. But I persevered—for Jill, for my sex life, for the long run. Whatever.

"*Scendere!*" called out Daniele as he headed his girls downhill. They all resumed talking and giggling to each other now that the pedaling was easier. That was the main difference in an Italian spin class. They never stopped talking, gossiping, trading recipes, flirting. It was a social scene more than a workout.

After fifteen minutes, my legs seemed to lighten. I raised the speed of the machine and the grade so that I could start to break a serious sweat. The TV was now showing an

MTV-type show with horrendous Italian pop music blaring out at me. But the beat was helpful. It moved me along.

Another quarter of an hour passed and I was flying. I got heated up enough that I actually had to peel off the cashmere sweater; this is an advanced workout for me. I actually felt . . . what's the word? I actually felt good. I made a mental note to be sure not to tell Jill, otherwise I would be committed for at least nine more sessions. But yes, this felt definitely good. I was alive! I felt strong. I could visualize the little pustules of plaque dislodging themselves from my artery walls. My heart was pounding steadily like the wonderful, trustworthy machine that it is. Oops. Don't say that. Don't curse yourself. Or there'll be an ambulance pulling up before you can say, "Jack LaLanne." But damn, I did feel good. And I felt something else, too. A familiar yearning feeling deep inside, bubbling up to the surface. I felt . . . what was that feeling? Oh, yeah. Hunger.

So what would it be? The seafood at Il Pescatore? Or that wild boar pasta in Pettino?

Fifteen

MARIANE IS JOJO'S MOTHER. When she visited Umbria a few years ago, JoJo introduced her to George, an American who had just moved to Umbria from Florence, where he had been running a wine-importing business. One thing led to another and—under JoJo's careful prodding—they were married a couple of years later at the Franciscan monastery high up on Monteluco. It pays to have a good agent for a daughter.

"George courted me with letters every day when I went back to New York, quoting Kant and Proust and all that. That didn't work with me," Mariane told me one day. "I'm just a girl who ran away to join the circus when I was fifteen."

But George pursued and a few months later invited her to fly back to Italy for a vacation.

"He told me he wanted to take me to see the wild almond blossoms in Sicily. Well, that sounded like a bit of all right."

So Mariane flew off to Sicily with just a few things

thrown in a suitcase because George had assured her it would be quite warm.

"It was fifty degrees—that's Fahrenheit—and no wild almond blossoms to be seen anywhere. But not very long after that we moved in together."

Mariane is George's fourth wife.

"And last," she added.

George started out publishing his family's newspaper in New Jersey. In a short time, he built a virtual empire, with more than twenty-five newspapers all over the country. At thirty he retired. He was an avid pilot, so he flew a plane over to East Africa and eventually started Wings for Progress, an airline that served previously unreachable communities in Kenya. Then he was off to Istanbul for five years. For journalism, he said.

"More like a journa*list*," added Mariane. "He was in fast pursuit of his second wife, I believe. Or third."

George got around.

Mariane is no slouch either. She left home as a teenager to be an actress at the Birmingham Rep, where she worked alongside Peter Brook in his very first professional job. She met Duncan Ross, her first husband—and JoJo's father—and eventually the two of them ran the Old Vic Theater School in Bristol. Then they emigrated to the States and ended up in Seattle, where Duncan—known as Bill—became the artistic director of the Seattle Rep. After his death, she bounced back and forth in various jobs between Seattle and New York—until that fateful visit to her daughter in Umbria, where she met George.

We had them over to the Rustico for dinner one night and they brought us a gift, a book of photography George had published on the Pian Grande, the vast glacial plain that lies six thousand feet above sea level at the foot of Monte Vettore. George, who knows a thing or two, enthralled us over dinner with stories and information about this otherworldly plain and about Castelluccio, the tiny hill town which is its one outpost of civilization. Mariane insisted that the only way to fully appreciate this remarkable area was to see it with her and George, so we made a plan for the following week.

On Wednesday, Jill, Caroline and I drove up to Bazzano, where they live. Bazzano—like many of the towns in the area—is split in two. There's Bazzano Superiore high up on the mountain, and Bazzano Inferiore below. It could give you a complex. After a tour of their exquisite house, we loaded up the car—George, it seems, never travels without a cooler filled with bottles of chilled Prosecco (the cooler plugs into the cigarette lighter of his SUV)—and set off over the mountain and down into the Valnerina.

The Valnerina is a completely different planet from the wide and agricultural Spoleto Valley. It's narrow and steep, its little hill towns seemingly impossible to get to, with no visible roads going in or out. It is also unimaginably beautiful. We drove farther east through Norcia, the Valnerina's largest and most famous town—birthplace of St. Benedict and the pork capital of Italy—and started climbing into the Sibillini Mountains. The mountains and the national park that surrounds them are named after Sybil, the prophetess who legend says was driven out of the underworld and into a cave in this wild remote mountain chain. We could fairly feel her eerie presence as the road became more and more remote and the temperature started dropping. As the car continued climbing we passed a ski lodge and noticed tall striped poles on the side of the road that George said were to measure the depth of the snow in winter.

Mariane and George

As we rounded a final bend in the road, both George and Mariane, normally loquacious, suddenly clammed up—like two little children with a secret they could barely keep. We drove in silence for a few more minutes and when we crested the hill we saw—stretched out below us—the vast expanse of the Pian Grande, fifteen kilometers across, surrounded by the snowcapped Sibillini, dominated by Monte Vettore, in whose crater grow the famous lentils of Castelluccio. It was a landscape from another planet. It was a landing field for spaceships from Mars. No photographs, no book, no stories could have prepared us for the size and scope of the beauty that spread out before us. And, all the way over on the other side of the plain, perched on a hill like a trusty old watchdog, sat tiny, falling-down Castelluccio—population around 150—as it's been sitting there, housing shepherds and lentil farmers, for over a thousand years.

We parked, got out of the car and tried to take it all in.

George opened the first bottle of Prosecco and poured us each a glass as we stood there, gaping.

After a while, we drove down to the flat plain. Distances were deceiving in such an immense space, and it was only when we reached the floor of the valley that things began to come into focus. There were vast flocks of sheep on both sides of the road, pushed by sheepdogs up and down the fields. There were no shepherds to be seen; the dogs knew exactly what to do on their own. Caroline asked if she could approach the dogs and George said that should be no problem, so we stopped the car about halfway across the plain and got out.

Caroline ran right into the middle of the flock—she has an instinct for animals and they for her. Three dogs came to her immediately, sniffing her out, and in no time they were on their backs having their bellies rubbed.

"Someone should take better care of them. They need to be washed and have their coats brushed."

Mariane explained that these dogs are workers, not pets, but Caroline would have none of it.

"You see how they love to be touched? They want to be cared for like everyone else."

We all backed away and watched from the road as our stubborn little Korean orphan lay on the ground, giving her own brand of unconditional love to these flea-bitten, mangy, ecstatically happy dogs, in the middle of literally hundreds of bleating sheep, on an endless plain of wildflowers, surrounded by snowcapped mountains. It was a sight.

We went for lunch in Castelluccio. Mariane and George are friends with the couple that run the Taverna Castelluccio and we were warmly welcomed and given the table by the

Caroline on the Pian Grande

window. They filled our glasses from bottles of George's Prosecco and told us what they were cooking that day. Polenta with house-made sausages; *minestra di farro*—a soup made from the speltlike grain that has been growing in this region since ancient times; fresh *tagliarini* with wild mushrooms from the mountains; lentils with sausages; a mixed grill featuring young lamb from the flock we had just been playing with—that was hard to get by Caroline. At least they weren't serving dog. And they strenuously recommended that we try their ricotta cheese, which was so fresh it was still warm, served drizzled with local honey. We got a plate of that to start and nearly ruined our appetite for the rest of lunch. The ricotta—literally "recooked" cheese— had a freshness that connected it in taste and smell to the milk of the animal it had just come from. And the sweet eucalyptus honey made an almost startling contrast. We smeared the cheese on fresh-baked Umbrian saltless bread, spooned the honey on top and washed it down with ice-cold Prosecco. Not a bad start to the meal.

I had the polenta for my *secondi,* with sausages and tomato sauce—as satisfying a dish as I've ever packed away—and a green salad from the garden. I'm not generally much of a salad eater—I think because most of the greens I've had put before me have been stale and tasteless and had to be tarted up with vinaigrettes or worse to have any taste at all. The surprise is that lettuce—fresh out of the ground—is delicious. It's succulent and sweet and needs— to my taste—just a little good olive oil as a complement. And maybe a sprinkle of salt. Two and half hours later— after getting to know George and Mariane a lot better, and they us—I finished up my meal with espresso: two cups, to keep myself awake after all that good food and wine.

Castelluccio is tiny. And its population is shrinking every year. As in many farm villages in Italy, the young people are drifting off to the cities and the old ways are dying off. George described what it's like there in the dead of winter— buried deep in snow and virtually unapproachable. No wonder its young people are running off. Then, George led us over to a promontory and described what happens to the plain in late June and early July—the spring comes late at these altitudes.

"There's a yellow flower that the locals call *ramacciole.* It's the bloom that precedes the fruit on the lentil plants. In the spring, there are wide swaths of them as far as you can see. And in between the lentils are fields of purple cornflowers alternated with swaths of red poppies. So this whole

Dancing on the Pian Grande

plain is like an immense, living, growing oil painting—like a fifteen-kilometer-long Rothko."

Today, Castelluccio's main industry is tourism. There are shops and stands that sell the famous products of the region—lentils, pecorino cheese, sausages, honey and *farro*—and we wandered around after lunch, shopping.

On the way back, we stopped again to check out the sheep and noticed a couple of other cars parked near the flock. When we got close to them, we heard loud music being piped out of one car's CD player—a wild folk-type music, almost Celtic, featuring drums and mountain pipes and soaring fiddles, not unlike the *pizzica-pizzica* we had danced the tarantella to in Puglia the year before. There were three couples—in their mid-sixties, perhaps—dancing in a makeshift conga line, waving their arms and whooping to the sky. Before anyone could blink, Jill—who will dance at the slightest provocation—was among them, instantly organizing the line into something more cohesive.

Under her lead, the merry band found the beat of the music and started dancing more as a group than as individual drunken sots. Her hands were on the shoulders of the woman in front of her. The man behind her—grinning like a fool—had both his hands cupped around her buttocks as the conga line wove between the wildflowers and the steaming mounds of sheep dip. Before long we were all dancing and whooping to the sky like idiots—except Caroline, who puts far more trust in dogs and sheep than she does in humans. The old guy behind Jill, who had taken one hand off her ass so that he could wave it up to the mountains, yelled at me across the circle, "*C'era Limoncello! C'era Limoncello!*" He was blaming their behavior on that sweet, subtly dangerous after-dinner liqueur. Apparently they had had a good lunch, too.

Sixteen

WE INVITED BRUNO AND MAYES over for dinner. We hadn't seen as much of them as we had some of our other new friends, partly because they're both busy—either off around the world somewhere doing a film, or in their studio in Trevi preparing to do one—but also, we decided, because they thought of us as the people who took their Rustico away. Of course, we'd paid them for it and all that, but we knew—Jill especially—that Mayes hadn't really been ready to let it go, and perhaps she was hesitant to come over and be a guest in what she still thought of as her house. It may not be logical, but there you are. So Jill and Caroline proposed that I cook dinner for them at the Rustico as a good way to get over this hump and see what kind of friendship could develop.

It's daunting to cook Italian food for an Italian—even more so to cook it for a Roman. Most Romans haven't accepted the fact that they don't still rule the civilized world, and Bruno is no exception. And whereas he might be willing to hear other opinions about politics or art or philosophy, he's very adamant—dare we say arrogant?—when it comes to *la cucina Italiana*. He's what they call in Italy a *buona forchetta,* which literally means "a good fork" but more loosely translates as one who knows how to handle himself at the table. He's also one of the world's great restaurant hounds—he can sniff out formidable feeds in places that most people don't know exist. Every Sunday he sets out with Mayes to discover his latest trattoria, or *osteria,* or taverna—usually far out into the Valnerina where sheep dot the hillside and the smell of *fertilizer naturale* drifts down from the mountains into the valley below. Usually it'll be what we in the States would call a roadhouse—a local tavern where the tables are packed with farmers, shopkeepers, shepherds . . . and Bruno. Mama's at the stove, Papa's at the bar and the food is purely and blissfully local.

I had cooked for him once before—a casual lunch that I threw together shortly after we got here. He came over to show me where things were—the fuse box, the garden tools, the propane tank—and I fed him a quick, little lunch. I served—audaciously—that most Roman of dishes: *pasta all'a-matriciana.* Except that I substituted the local Umbrian pasta, *strangozzi,* for the traditional *bucattini* and finished it with *parmigiano* instead of *pecorino Romano*—which to a Roman is as blasphemous as missing lunch. But I was confident. I'd been cooking this dish for twenty-five years—ever since I tasted it on my first sojourn in Rome. And doing it here in Italy where I can get house-made *guanciale,* the famous Canarra onions and tomatoes from my own garden made it virtually foolproof. And even though Bruno pointed out my substitutions immediately, he was smiling broadly when he helped himself to his second portion. He even called his mother in Rome: "Mom, you won't believe what this guy did. . . ."

So for this dinner—when we were trying to woo them—I decided to make the dinner as authentic as possible; no profit in turning off Bruno at the outset. I decided to give us all a break from Umbrian cuisine and do a pasta Bolognese; then a simple salad of *rucola* and *parmigiano;* then a couple of chickens—flattened, marinated and grilled over the fire. I had already made the Bolognese sauce the day before with fresh ground *vitellone* I got from the butcher in Pissignano. *Vitellone* is older veal—just before it's considered beef. There's *vitello, vitellini, vitellone*—all different ages of the calf. Vitellini, it's been explained to me, is when the calf is still suckling from the mother; vitello is when it's both suckling and grazing; and vitellone is when it's completely weaned and subsisting on grass. The butcher and I had a consultation as he ground the meat, adding just the right amount of *grasso* (fat) into the mix so that I got the maximum amount of taste. Then I picked up a couple of carrots, an onion and two stalks of celery from Gloria, the *ortafrutta* lady in Campello—you can buy celery one stalk at a time here; they just snap off what you need—and some fresh tomatoes which I peeled and seeded for the sauce. I used a Grechetto, the local white wine, and the freshest milk from a local cow. It was to be the best Bolognese I've ever made.

There's a fresh pasta store right down the road from us that's owned and run by a woman named Laura—who happens to be the wife of Domenico, who takes care of our garden. We found him through his aunt Vittoria, who is our cleaning lady—plus our fresh egg supplier, our source for seasoned firewood and our identifier of the wild herbs and greens that are growing all over the stone walls that surround our land. She is the person we go to when we need to connect with any- and everything local.

I drove down to Laura's place and was waited on first by her daughter. I told her I had made a Bolognese and couldn't decide whether I wanted to serve it over tagliatelle or tortellini. She reached down and took out a tray of very freshly made tortellini, stuffed with veal, cheese and herbs, and that decision was taken care of. Then I asked her if she knew where I could get great chickens. She said she'd have to ask her dad. A few moments later Domenico came out from the back with a big smile and a "*Come va?*" and asked how he could help.

"I'm looking for some great chickens—*nostrano,*" which means fresh and local. He shrugged and shook his head. He didn't know where to send me. Whereas all the butchers had good fresh chickens, they would have been raised on poultry farms and, although they would be far superior to anything we could find in the States, they wouldn't be the backyard, dirt-scratching, dinner-scraps-fed chicken I was looking for. Then he had an idea and told me to wait while he went in the back to talk to Laura. A few minutes later she came out—also with a smile, and a long string of incomprehensible Italian words.

She asked what I was going to do with the chickens, and I told her "*diavolo*"—grilled flat, with pepper, over wood coals. She raised her finger for me to wait and helped another man who had just come in. When he left and the store was momentarily empty, she whispered that she had chickens for me—but that I mustn't tell anyone where I got them; she wasn't, after all, in the chicken business. After I was sworn to secrecy, she went in the back and brought out two chickens—*gelato;* which sounds like chicken-flavored ice cream but just means they've been frozen solid. These chickens were local to the point of being members of her family; they'd grown up with her kids. They were also the weirdest looking poultry I have ever seen. Wrapped in plastic wrap, sticking out of the shopping bag, they looked too long and thin to be chickens; they looked more like jackrabbits. She told me to soak them in water, white wine and lemon to defrost them.

I paid her for the pasta and the birds and headed down to the piazza to get some fresh *rucola* from Gloria. Now I was ready to start cooking.

Once the chickens had thawed, I was able to get a good look at them. Their legs were at least a foot and a half long, and their bodies were leaner and more compact than the chickens I'd formerly hung out with. They seemed to be built for speed—though not enough speed to escape being dinner.

I split them down the back, removed the backbone, chopped off the tips of the wings and pressed the chickens against the board until I heard a satisfying crack. Now they were flat enough to cook evenly on the grill. I salted them, bathed them in olive oil and rosemary, then ground rather more pepper than usual over them and rubbed it in. A lot of black pepper is what makes *diavolo* so diavo-lish. Then I covered them and put them in the fridge for a couple of hours to let the flavors seep in.

That evening there wasn't that much work left to do. I slowly reheated the Bolognese—which would be even better having spent a day in the fridge to sit and pull itself together—and started a wood fire in our *camino* in the living room.

Our fireplace is raised about two feet off the floor—there's wood storage below—and I can comfortably get my eyes even with the cooking surface. The grill rig has four different levels so that I can instantly adjust the relationship between the heat and the meat. And I can add smaller twigs (preferably clippings from the olive trees), which give an almost instant rush of very high temperature when I need that.

I brought my long, thin, Modigliani-like chickens up to room temperature in their marinade. I set them on a rack so that they could drip off the excess oil, and when the wood coals were perfect I set them side by side, skin side down, onto the grill. Every ten minutes or so, I held my hand over the fire at the level of the grill to get a feeling of the intensity of the heat. If I felt the fire was flagging, I added some sticks and got them going with an old bellows that I'd bought at a flea market. The bellows also blew the dust off the old coals and kept them lively.

Bruno and Mayes arrived with two bottles of wine that they had siphoned off from a huge jug that Bruno kept in their basement. The jug was filled on a regular basis at a wine cooperative somewhere in Montefalco. I asked Bruno if he could introduce me to the people at the cooperative and he smiled and said, "Sure," but I could see in his eyes that this wouldn't happen anytime soon. Some secrets you take to the grave.

Bruno and I took our glasses of wine into the living room to watch the chickens slowly grill on the fire while the girls got to know each other in the kitchen. Caroline, who is a formidable sous-chef, tended the sauce and started the pasta in the boiling water. Jill—known internationally for her lettuce drying—worked on the salad. Mayes helped set the table. And the little house filled with the sound of their chatter and laughter. Bruno and I sat, sipped and appreciated the palpable glow that can emanate from three such exquisitely beautiful women.

Mayes and Bruno

"You know, you could really lighten this place up," he said, his eyes darting around the room. "I had plans to knock this wall down so that it opened up to the new section. And then maybe move the fireplace more to the middle."

Knock the wall down? It's 350 years old; I'm going to knock it down? "Sure, why not?"

He grinned. "You got a pen?"

I fetched a pen and paper and he started sketching. I watched over his shoulder as our dark little *salotto* turned into a gracious, sun-filled room with space for a long dining table with all our friends around it, and comfy chairs by the fire. There was a curved staircase in the new part that led to a new master bedroom upstairs—also equipped with a fire-place. He did all this with a few quickly drawn lines on paper.

"You want a Jacuzzi?" That grin again.

I started salivating with the possibilities.

"Martin said we might—"

"Yeah, Martin's good," he said dismissively, his eyes moving around the room again.

Martin's an architect; Bruno designs movie sets. Martin deals with real houses; Bruno makes pictures—beautiful pictures.

"Pasta's ready!" Caroline from the kitchen.

We sat down to steaming bowls of tortellini Bolognese, spooning freshly grated *parmigiano* on top. I opened the next bottle and filled everyone's glass. Bruno tasted the pasta, and then tasted again.

"Wow, this is the real thing. You got it right."

I blushed with pleasure.

"You know, when Mayes and I first got married, she cooked pasta for me."

"I had to learn Italian cooking immediately," said Mayes in her Mexican-accented English. "Or he would have divorced me."

"So I'm sitting there," said Bruno, "waiting for my first dinner from my new wife—spaghetti carbonara, which she knows I've loved since I was a little kid in Rome. She brings it very proudly to the table and I see immediately it has little peas in it, and prosciutto instead of pancetta and . . . I couldn't believe it!!"

"You said it was great," piped in Mayes.

"Yeah, it was fine, but it wasn't carbonara! Carbonara is pancetta, eggs, cheese, spaghetti. *Basta cosi!* I told her she could call it anything she wants—call it *pasta va fa'nculo*—just don't tell me I'm having carbonara!"

Pasta va fa'nculo, by the way, can be roughly translated as "pasta up your ass."

"So, the next day," continues Bruno, "she brings me this pasta—it had like American ketchup on it and . . . I don't know what else. And I asked her, 'What's this?' And she looks right into my eyes and tells me, 'That's *pasta va fa'nculo.*'

"I never criticized her cooking again."

We had more tortellini; we filled the wineglasses again; we told stories about past cooking disasters, which quickly reminded me to check on my chickens in the fireplace. Then Jill cleared the pasta bowls and set the plates for our *secondi,* while I cut up the chickens—done just fine, thank God—into serving pieces. Mayes and Caroline talked about taking a hike together the next morning and Jill said that she would join them. That meant the girls could now eat the next course without guilt.

When Jill asked them about work, Bruno said that he was becoming much more selective these days—it was becoming harder for him to leave the home he'd created here in Umbria, and to be separated from Mayes. She shook her head resolutely.

"No. We need the money. We will still take the jobs." Her forehead wrinkled with seriousness, which made her look all the more childlike. "And not just for the money. I love my work."

I looked at Bruno; he smiled back and shrugged. He had made his success, over and over. Now, he seemed to be saying, he was ready for the next phase of his life. "But yeah, more money wouldn't be a bad thing, either."

We all laughed. I felt a strong pull for this guy. It had been Bruno and Mayes—as much as the Rustico, the countryside and Italy itself—that had attracted us in the beginning, that first day under the pergola. The dinner had done its job. *Il ghiaccio era rotto.* The ice was broken.

Seventeen

OUR LAST WEEK AT THE RUSTICO came as a shock. I
had been in complete denial about our departure until we
started getting invitations to farewell dinners.

"Who's leaving?" I asked.

We were feted pretty much every night. Martin and
Karen had us up to meet friends of theirs—some from Germany, some from the States. They cooked a Thai dinner that
Martin had shopped for at the Mercato Coperto near the
railway station in Rome. It's part of the outdoor market at
the Piazza Vittorio and famous for its food products from all
over the world. So, lemongrass, Thai chilies, fish sauce—all
very un-Umbrian. Bruce and JoJo invited us over for some
trout grilled over wood in the fireplace that was as good as
any fish I've ever tasted. Bruce has a way with wood-fire
cookery. Mayes cooked us a dinner of tagliatelle with porcini,
proving that she had come a long way from the days of *pasta va
fa'nculo*. Then the whole gang hosted us for a farewell blast at
the Palazzaccio. This merry band of expats and transplanted
Italians party at the slightest provocation, and our departure to

the States was excuse enough for a weeklong celebration, one dinner spilling into the next. I was going to miss these people sorely.

Caroline was actually eager to get back to Mill Valley. She had her triathlon team waiting for her, all sweated up and ready to go; she had a new job about to start that needed her attention, and any number of suitors panting for the chance to take her out on the town. She was also getting nervous about all the pasta she was putting away.

Jill and I, on the other hand, couldn't figure out why we were going back. Our life in beautiful Mill Valley was very pleasant, to be sure, but we felt like we were leaving one vacation to go to another. Where was the work part? All our new friends in Umbria were artists of one kind or another and they were as passionate about their work as they were about living the good life. They made us aware that we, too, had some artistic muscles that needed flexing. It was time to get back to work. Our eight-year sojourn in Northern California had been great for us: it had helped us transition from burnt-out TV stars into human beings. But now we needed to make another transition: from human beings—a state we were never fully comfortable with—into actors again.

While we were turning this over, we got an offer to do a play at the Marin Theater Company, the professional troupe right around the corner from our house. It was a new play by a young writer out of New York, and we leapt at it. I had a wonderful time getting back on stage and, after knocking a little rust off, felt quite good about the whole thing. But Jill was a veritable revelation. She took the role between her teeth like a pit bull and didn't let up until it was hers completely. She was extraordinary. I couldn't help thinking that her performance needed to be seen by a broader, more theater-savvy audience. It was work easily worthy of New York.

I called our agent in L.A. and told him he had to come up and see the show—that he had never seen Jill do anything like this. He turned me down flat. He said that it was pilot season and that he could do us more good by staying down in L.A. trying to get us back on TV. I tried to explain to him that he couldn't adequately represent Jill without first seeing her performance in this play—that there was a whole aspect of her work he had never seen. He had no idea what I was talking about—and no intention of coming to see the play. I started to feel more strongly than ever that we were living in the wrong state, on the wrong coast, perhaps in the wrong country.

The food thing wasn't working either. Which for me is basic. The first day back from Italy, we decided to go to a favorite Chinese restaurant in downtown Mill Valley. We hadn't had Chinese food in six weeks so, with Caroline, we walked into town for lunch. We sat down, ordered and twenty-five minutes later we were standing outside on the street corner, blinking in the sunshine, wondering what the hell had just happened. It certainly wasn't lunch. Lunch is two and a half hours followed by a nap; lunch is the focal point of the day, not a quick stop at the filling station.

The whole food situation was puzzling. In the States, Jill can't eat garlic or onions; bread and pasta are no-nos; and she tries to stay away from dairy products. She has a delicate digestion. In Italy she has no problem with any of those things. She eats it all, happily, and her digestion works just fine. So, what's the difference? Attitude? Lifestyle? Certainly. But there's also the thousand-year-old tradition of eating well in Italy; there's *terreno,* the soil that things are grown in; and there's the crucial question of freshness.

In Mill Valley we shop—as do all the dutiful yuppies—at one of those health-oriented megastores with dazzling Disneyland displays of produce, condiments and packaged goods that all proclaim themselves to be "organic." Well, they may well be organic, and they may be "artisinally grown"—but they damn well aren't fresh. The produce—which looks great—tastes like it's been on a truck for two weeks. Its vitality is gone. It's all show.

"*Nostrano*" is a word that pops up on hand-written signs at local *alimentari* and roadside stands in Umbria. It comes from the word "*nostro,*" which means "ours." If the ricotta they're selling today is proclaimed *nostrano,* it was made in the neighborhood and it's still warm. When the porcini start popping up from under the oak trees, they're suddenly everywhere—fresh and bursting with flavor. All the restaurants are serving them—in pastas, blanketing roasted meats, grilled on their own like steaks, glistening with olive oil. And the fun is that this can only be happening now, on the day they pop up—and here, from under trees you can see on the hillsides, just up the road from where you're eating them.

"*Nostrano*" is also used when talking about meat. The pork we eat in Umbria is from pigs that could have walked to the butcher shop where they're sold. They're neighborhood pigs. They know people you know. Same with the wines—they grow in vineyards that you can see out the window. They're grown to be sipped with the food that grows near them. That's why they go down so well. *Nostrano.*

The problem in the States is that the Caesar salad with grilled chicken in San Jose is the same one you get in Providence; the arugula salad with baked goat cheese is rubber-stamped and mass-produced until it appears on restaurant menus in all fifty states. It's Mall Food—as ubiquitous as the Gap, or Radio Shack, or T.G.I. Friday's.

Yes, there are farmers' markets in the Bay Area. Famously. It is, after all, the land of Alice Waters and the California food revolution. And yes, you can get fresh produce and products. But they don't come cheaply; fresh food is for rich people. Frustrated with the food we were getting, we took the advice of friends and went into San Francisco to shop at the market at the Ferry Building on the Embarcadero. We found some nice grilling peppers—six pretty specimens: fourteen dollars; wild mushrooms that looked good for pasta: a medium-sized bag, twenty- two bucks; a cheese store with beautiful cheeses made artisinally in western Marin—we picked out one that looked good: eighteen dollars for a cheese the size of my fist. Before getting as far as meats or fish for the main course, we'd dropped seventy-five bucks for a meal for three.

I threw a dinner party for some friends, thinking I'd show off what I'd learned in Italy. I'd make a little *pasta alla Norcia*—sausages, cream and porcini—then a simple mixed grill of meats marinated in the Umbrian manner and cooked over wood; then I'd finish it off with a *rucola* salad and *parmigiano*. Then one of the guests called and reminded me that she ate no meat. Okay. I changed the menu to spaghetti *vongole,* scampi on the grill and the *rucola* with *parmigiano*. Then another guest called to remind me that she believed in food combining—which means that she didn't eat protein and carbs in the same meal. Fine. I changed the menu. I'd roast some chickens, maybe stuff them with some garlic-scented croutons—oops, can't do that. Okay, chickens, grilled with olive oil that we brought back—maybe a mixed grill with ribs and sausages as well as the chicken oops, no meat; then just the *rucola* salad with *parmigiano*. Yeah, that would work. Then a third guest called to remind me that she was a vegan. Which means she eats nothing that ever lived or breathed, or dairy, or. . . .

I ached for Umbria. I e-mailed JoJo and Martin almost daily, getting news from the gang and negotiating whether we were going to go ahead with our *"amplificazione"*—the enlargement of the Rustico. The obvious impediment was money. It would cost approximately what we'd paid for the house originally. And, of course, construction always costs more than planned. Especially because we would have to open up 350-year-old walls to connect the two sections, and you never know what you're going to find when you do that—there could be an old monk in there. JoJo counseled patience.

"Maybe you've already got what you came for. A perfect little two-bedroom cottage—no room for guests. Over and done. You can put your friends up at the Castello. Much less of a pain in the ass anyway."

Martin urged us to go forward with the project.

"If you don't do it now, there's every chance you will never be allowed to do it. The rules are tightening; the permits are more and more scarce. And a four-bedroom house with a pool in the olive groves will be worth a lot more money than it will cost you to build."

I knew this to be true. It would be a good investment. Even JoJo agreed with that.

"Sure, you would have what everyone wants and no one can find. No question about that. It just depends on what *you* want—and what you can afford. But nobody ever lost money building in Umbria—not in my time here, anyway."

So, after a lot of thought, we made two moves that would turn out to radically change the direction of our life—again. We called Martin and JoJo and told them to go ahead with the *amplificazione;* and, to help pay for it, we decided to make a concerted effort to get back in the game— the acting game, that is. This meant spending more time in L.A. or New York. Or both. We'd have to do it on a commuting basis, because we didn't really want to live in either of those places—L.A. had never been our town, really, and New York . . . well, Jill didn't feel she could live there again on a full-time basis. She had gotten too used to redwood trees and hiking trails in the woods, to the natural beauty of Northern California, to her full complement of alternative health care specialists. No, New York was too much hustle and bustle for her now. We'd try to commute when we got a job.

We called Judy Katz, our longtime friend and publicist in New York. We told her that we needed to get back to work in order to support our Italy habit. She'd been trying to get us back to New York for eighteen years, so she delightedly volunteered to cast about to find an agent who would want to take us on even though we would have to fly in from California for auditions. She said lots of actors went back and forth from L.A. to New York, so why not from Mill Valley to New York? She'd get right on it.

The work in Umbria would proceed in two stages. First, before we went back in the spring, we would have the contractor prepare the old Rustico for its eventual merging with the new part of the house. This would entail knocking three large holes through its three-foot-thick walls—one in the living room/dining room, which would connect to the new entryway and *salotto;* one in our bedroom directly above, making what was a window into French doors that would open onto the new terrace; and a third in the kitchen, which would create a pantry that I thought we needed to make the old kitchen work.

This work would proceed immediately and be finished by spring so that we could live in the old house while the work on the new section got under way. We booked our flight for the first of May and made a plan for Alison, our daughter, to fly over and join us there.

Eighteen

WE RETURNED TO THE RUSTICO IN MAY and experienced early spring in Umbria for the first time. It was a dazzler. The mountains above the house were still in winter, snowcapped and majestic, but at our level—about 1,200 feet—it was all wildflowers and trees in bud. The Rustico had survived its onslaught, although Martin later confided that when they opened up the hole for the door in the living room, they discovered a less than adequate foundation under the old wall. For a nervous day and a half, while the masons frantically jacked up the house and poured cement in under the old foundation, we were in real danger of losing the entire north wall of the house. We were grateful not to have heard about it until well after the situation had been taken care of.

I had worried that we were crazy to tamper with this picture-perfect cottage, but now that we saw it opened up a bit, we realized it hadn't been perfect at all. Now the little house had light streaming in from every direction. With the window in the new pantry we could finally see what we were doing in the kitchen; our bedroom was now a sun-filled, gracious room with French doors opening out onto what would eventually be a terrace (until that was built, however, had we opened the doors too quickly we would have plunged twenty feet to the yard below). And the living/dining room, which had been the darkest room in the house, now had beautiful glass and chestnut doors that would connect to our new entrance foyer and multiwindowed living room.

In medieval times, when the house was built, people didn't want light streaming in. They wanted to sit by the fire, in the dark, and eat their gruel. They wanted a house to protect them—from the elements and from their enemies—not to be open and light and airy. But we weren't living in the Middle Ages. We were Californians—free in mind and spirit—and we rarely, if ever, ate gruel.

The first day back is always a marathon. After flying all night—and gaining nine hours against the clock—we forced ourselves to stay awake and try to make it through to a reasonable bedtime hour. So we planned a party for ourselves at the Palazzaccio, rounding up all the usual suspects for an Umbrian feast before we put ourselves to bed, our tummies full and happy. It was a warm enough night to eat out in the back garden of the restaurant, and we all gathered around one of the big picnic tables—Bruce and JoJo, Martin and Karen, Bruno and Mayes, George and Mariane—and listened to Danila chant her traditional opening number.

"*Acqua—naturale e frizzante. Vino rosso, vino bianco.*"

We all turned our glasses over as the pitchers of wine and water arrived and were passed around. George, of course, insisted on bottles of Prosecco as well. There was a new batch of kittens that were climbing up the pergola poles to escape the attention of the family kids, who pursued them relentlessly; platters of bruschetta appeared, the toasted, oiled bread covered variously with truffles and mushrooms, liver paste or tomatoes and basil; JoJo and Martin continued their argument over Fidelio, even though he was long out of the picture; Bruce showed me a brochure for the high-speed Internet connection that had just become available; Bruno had just bought a new pile of rocks that he was developing high up in Campello Alto; Karen, Mayes and Jill made a date to go to the gym together. Plates of pasta arrived—*ravioli Laetizia, strongozzi tartufo, spaghetti Benedettina*. We were home.

Jill and I woke up the next morning and tiptoed through the house, planning what we would do when it was done— furnishings and lamps, a piano, a chair by the fire. We sat out under the pergola and had our breakfast, listening to the seemingly endless variety of birds. The birds ate the bugs, the bugs ate us, we ate our breakfast, and all was right with the world.

Martin and JoJo came by for a meeting that afternoon and we went over the plans and the schedule. They had finally agreed on a contractor for the second phase of construction, which would start on the day we left—a fellow named Nicola from Naples, who worked with his two brothers, Enzo and Ivano. Neither JoJo nor Martin had worked with them before, but they had come highly recommended. We were delighted just to see the two of them agree with each other.

Alison was due in a few days for a two-week visit. This was momentous, as we hadn't spent that much time together—just the three of us—since Max was born twenty years earlier. She was twelve at the time and we had—stupidly, patronizingly—asked her if she wanted a baby brother. She'd leveled a look at us and blurted an adamant and resounding "No!" Max, who had already been conceived at that point, couldn't be sent back for another model, and although the two kids have grown quite close over the years, our daughter has never again fully trusted her parents.

Alison is a singular girl. She's had an independent spirit since she was a kid, and growing up has just served to strengthen it. After she had been living on her own for four years of college, she came out to stay with us in L.A., and it didn't take us long to realize that we couldn't go back to the old parent/child relationship; that toothpaste was out of the tube and there was no putting it back in. On her second night in town, she and some friends took off to Vegas for three days without bothering to mention it to us. A week later—after some spirited family meetings—we helped her move into her own place, where she's been ever since. So this visit would be a test—the three of us together in a tiny cottage for twelve days.

Alison's a cook—a chef. She tried the acting business for a few years and finally got fed up with the rejection. She went back to school, got her chef's license, went into business for herself and is doing quite well. Both our kids have gone into professions that are manifestations of their parents' fantasies: Max is the professional musician that Jill always dreamed of being; Alison is the professional chef I fancied I'd like to be.

For her first night in Umbria, we had Bruno and Mayes over and Alison made some biscotti for dessert. They are a specialty of hers—double-baked with chocolate, hazelnut and dried cherries. Bruno couldn't get over them. He said they were the best biscotti he had ever tasted and took all the leftovers home with him. Mayes reported that they were gone the next day and put in an order for more. Alison beamed.

I had grilled some steaks that night that got her attention, and she asked the next day if she could take a field trip with me to my butcher. I told her this was complicated because I now had three butchers, none of whom knew about the others. This poly-amorous situation started with my relationship with Lauro, my first love, the butcher on the road to the station in Spoleto. Then I heard about Ugo, who's right in our little town of Campello. Ugo is an artisan, a maker of prosciutto in the old manner, whom I had heard about from Karen. He speaks in the Umbrian dialect and is as shy as I am, so our relationship was still tentative. Then there's Corrado, the pork specialist in Pissignano, who's like a new hottie, tempting me to stray.

We started our tour with Lauro, who, we learned upon arrival, had retired after forty years in the same location and handed over the business to his son, Fabio. Alison was immediately enchanted. Not only is Fabio a good-looking guy, but he also has his dad's charm. A visit to Lauro was always a cooking lesson, a flirtation and a therapy session all rolled up together. And Fabio, young though he is, can deliver like his pop. Alison asked about cuts of beef, which are very different in Italy, and Fabio gave her an anatomy lesson. Then—again like his dad—he tempted us with a taste of mortadella, which we bought; then a taste of *coralina,* which we bought; then a taste of *porchetta,* which was irresistible as well.

On the way home, our packages of goodies stowed in the car, we decided to stop at Ugo's place. His shop is modest, old-fashioned compared with Lauro's sparkling emporium. When we walked in, through the beads that hang over the door to keep out the flies, there was no one around. From the ceiling, thirty or so prosciuttos hung like Christmas decorations.

"*Buongiorno?*" I called out.

After a moment, Ugo appeared. He was in a leather apron and his face was flushed with exertion. He looked a little embarrassed, as always.

"*Queste la figlia,*" I told him, introducing Alison.

He flushed again and wiped his hands very carefully on a towel.

"Ugo," he said. "*Un piacere.*" And he took her hand in both of his and bowed.

"*Tu sei occupato?*" I asked if he was too busy for us.

"*No, no. Sono dentro. Con I prosciutti, facendo un massaggio.*"

When I frowned with confusion, he smiled and waved us to the door that led to the back of his shop. He was suddenly courtly—clearly because Alison was there. It seems that all butchers like to flirt with the girls. I whispered to her that I thought he had just told us that he was in the back massaging his prosciutto, but that maybe I hadn't gotten it quite right.

The back of his shop is immense—four or five times the area of the part in front. It has three rooms: one has a great fireplace that takes up the whole wall, and another is a walk-in, refrigerated space.

"Is this where you make the prosciutto?" Alison asked in English.

"*Si, si, tutti qui.*" He seemed to understand her perfectly.

He took us into the refrigerated room and opened a drawer that was about twelve feet long and three feet deep. It was filled with salt.

"*Primo si mette i prosciutti in un bagno di sale.*"

Ugo slicing prosciutto

"First," I translated, "he puts the ham in a bath of salt."

"For how long?" asked Alison.

I started to translate, but Ugo somehow understood. I decided to shut up and let them work it out on their own. She spoke in English; he spoke in his thick Umbrian dialect; and they did just fine.

"*Per un mese.*" A month in the salt. And then he explained that every few days he massages the salt into the hams, so that it permeates the skin. That's what he was doing when we arrived.

Then, after the month passes, he washes off the salt and rubs on a mixture of wine, herbs and a lot of pepper and hangs the hams from the ceiling for three more months. This allows them to slowly release their excess moisture. Then he "closes them up," which means he coats them with rendered pork fat—taken from under the ribs, the tastiest part—and encloses them completely. The covered hams are then hung in the fireplace to slowly smoke—for four more months.

At this point, Alison's eyes were as wide as saucers and Ugo was gaining confidence with each step he was describing. Next, he cleans the fat off and attaches a wooden tag on each ham inscribed with the date it was finished and then hangs them up from the ceiling again for at least two years. After that they graduate to the front of the shop, where they're ready to be sliced for the customers. He explained with pride that the prosciutto we get in the States—all of it—is produced with machines and that the process takes less than three months, start to finish. So, in essence, we have never tasted real prosciutto. Which is exactly what we did next.

Back in the front room, Ugo carved a slice for Alison. He uses a thin carving knife that looks like it's been around for generations. After a few quick strokes on the honing steel, he began to slowly saw the prosciutto, starting away from his body, cutting in the direction of his heart, so that he looks very much like a cellist—playing Brahms, perhaps. He handed Alison the perfect slice and waited.

"Oh. My. God," she said in Californian cadence.

Then Ugo moved to another, smaller ham on the slicing counter. He explained that this one is from the *spalla*, or shoulder, whereas the classic prosciutto is from the upper leg. This ham was darker, purplish in color and looked to have been aged much longer. We both tasted a slice. It was stronger, saltier and much more potent.

"*Sarebbe buono in una pasta,*" I ventured. Ugo lit up.

"*Si! In una pasta, si!*"

I immediately envisioned some penne in a light cream

sauce with some sautéed zucchini, grated *parmigiano*—and dotted with flecks of this dark, salty, delicious ham.

We bought some of each of the two prosciuttos. We quietly watched him slice; you can't be in a hurry at Ugo's. When he was done and we had paid up—not expensive, mind you—he asked me where we lived. When I told him we had bought a house just out of town and explained where the Rustico was, he lit up again.

"*C'e un forno!*"

Yes, I said. There is an oven.

He told us that our oven is much revered in this area. It has been there for over four hundred years—long before the little house was built—and was the community oven where the women would come every week to bake bread. There was emotion in his eyes.

We walked to the car and Alison carried the packages of ham like the treasures they were.

"So, Pops," she said.

I looked over at her.

"I think I'm going to marry an Italian butcher."

Which would be just fine with me.

Nineteen

WE TOOK ALISON TO ROME before she flew back to
L.A. She had lived there with us some twenty-eight years
before when we were making a movie and we wanted to
reconnect her with some memories—and some dear
friends—from all those years ago.

One memory etched forever in all our psyches was when
we decided to put her in school for the time we were there.
There is an American Overseas School in Rome and we enrolled Alison, who was seven years old and itching for some
kids her own age. On her first morning of school, the bus
picked her up right outside our apartment in Trastevere and
we waved her off confidently. That afternoon, Jill and I
waited at the same corner to meet the bus. Right on time,
we watched it coming up the street; we watched it arrive on
our corner, and there was Alison with her bright face in the
window, waving; and then we watched it pass us by without
slowing down and head off into the bowels of Rome, carrying our now screaming little girl to God knows where. I
took off at a dead run, Jill yelling encouragement, Alison

wailing in the window, the bus picking up speed. (I could still run in those days.) Five blocks later, the bus finally stopped at a traffic light and I caught up to it, throwing myself in front of it, sacrificing my body for my little girl. It was all very Italian.

So we revisited Trastevere and the sight of the great school bus chase. We went to the little pizza place right off the Piazza del Popolo, where Alison and I had eaten almost every night after Jill went back to New York. We visited the studio on the Palatine Hill where the movie had been shot. And we visited the Rotunnos.

Peppino and Graziolina Rotunno have been our friends for over three decades. Peppino was the director of photography on the movie and he brought his family down to Calabria for the first two weeks of shooting before we all moved back to Rome to complete the film. His wife, Graziolina, an artist whose exquisite paintings we have been collecting since we first met, and their daughter, Carmen, who is Alison's age, were along for the trip. Carmen and Alison took to each other immediately and, through them, the two families began a friendship that has managed to survive time and distance and all the other things that make people drift apart over the years.

So, the night before Alison flew back to L.A., Graziolina insisted on cooking for us at their apartment. Carmen, who is now married with two babies, would be there with her husband. She and Alison would get to see each other for the first time since they were kids.

Graziolina is almost as wonderful a cook as she is a painter. She was actually my first teacher of Italian cooking, back in the seventies. After Jill, and then Alison, left for the States, I still had three more months of work on the movie, and the Rotunnos took pity and had me to dinner on a regular basis. I'd hang out in the kitchen with Graziolina and watch as she effortlessly sautéed the chicken and vegetables for a cacciatore. And she took me step by step through my first risotto, which for me is still the most magical cooking process.

Our reunion dinner was a great success. The food, of course, was wonderful. Alison and Carmen—after warily eyeing each other's adult incarnation—connected again and remembered old times on the movie set. But what was all too evident was the difficulty we were having with the language barrier. Graziolina spoke the best English of the Italians, and she helped translate when things got sticky, but it was difficult to maintain a flow to the evening. Carmen's husband, Andrea, a young, successful attorney in Rome, had learned all his English from the lyrics of American rock and roll songs. So, whenever a word or a phrase came up that he understood, he sang the next line. We got a lot of laughs from it, but I can't say we got to know him as well as we would have liked. Carmen and Alison had had a much easier time communicating when they were seven than they now did as adults. There were long pauses as both of them tacitly acknowledged the futility of trying to get into a real conversation.

And most frustrating of all was talking with Peppino. He showed us a book that had just been published—a beautiful book with photographs—of scenes from the films of Fellini that had never been seen by the public, that had ended up on the cutting room floor. And Peppino, who had shot many of these films, was prominent in the book. There were pictures of him as a young man, working on the set with the Maestro, and he was recalling stories for us of Fellini, Mastroianni and many others. And we ached to be able to understand him better. He's retired now, but busier than ever. He teaches cinematography at Cinecitta and heads up the movement to preserve all the great Italian films of the past. His career reaches back through the golden days of Italian film to its early days, when he apprenticed as a camera assistant. He has stories to tell about all of it and we couldn't really understand them—not the subtleties; not the character nuances.

The one great language breakthrough we had that night was when we wanted something—which is usually the case. We asked Carmen if she knew about great places to shop for furniture for our house. She's a gold mine of information because she shops all over Rome for props and furniture for the theater pieces she designs. Graziolina got a pen and paper and Carmen dictated a list. And if we didn't understand her, we made her slow down and repeat it. The list would take us all over Rome, so Peppino fetched a map that would help us see where we were going.

After dinner, we hugged and kissed good-bye, making a promise to improve our Italian before our next dinner together. We decided to walk through the streets of Rome for a while so that Alison could get her last taste of Italy, and when we were about to cross the Tiber, not far from the Piazza del Popolo, Jill stopped and told us to listen.

"It's James, isn't it?"

And sure enough, we could hear the unmistakable sound of James Taylor, singing, "How sweet it is to be loved by you. . . ."

We followed the music, which led us into the piazza, which was filled with ten thousand or so Italians, swaying to the music of the free, live concert. We joined them, quietly sang along and thought back to our beach house days, when we pitched in with a bunch of other couples—young and out of work like us—to rent a dilapidated fraternity house on Fairfield Beach in Connecticut. Alison was a kid. We were kids. And James was our music.

This had been a good visit with Alison. Italy would be a place for us to come together—as adults—with both our children.

The next day—after Alison flew off—Jill and I charged around Rome in a shopping frenzy. Following Carmen's instructions, we went first to a shop in Prati that specialized in furniture from different parts of Asia. Since we couldn't afford to fill the house with antiques, we thought we'd mix things up a bit—some new, some old, some Italian, some not. We'd always furnished our houses this way. We eyed a set of lamps that we thought might go well in our new bedroom. But we had promised ourselves we wouldn't buy anything until the house was closer to being finished, so we just fantasized.

The next store on Carmen's list was an ultramodern emporium with fantastic Italian designs that we tried to imagine in our little Rustico. Fun to look at, but not for us. Then we wandered over to a little street off the Piazza Navona called Via Governo Vecchio that was filled with shops of every conceivable style. There were oriental carpet shops, expensive antiques, junk stores with hidden treasures, lamp shops and furniture makers, as well as clothing boutiques and shoe stores—and Baffetto, the best pizza in Rome. Governo Vecchio is a shopper's paradise, and we spent the rest of the morning wandering from one fabulous shop to another until we found the one on Carmen's list. It's a store that specializes in imports from Bali, Singapore and other parts of Asia, as well as the creations of some very individual designers from Italy and other parts of Europe. It's an eclectic collection that appealed to our taste immediately. And our budget. There was a dining table that caught my eye as I came through the door. It was carved from a single, immense slab of wood—teak, I think—and was more like a sculpture than a piece of furniture. As I drooled over it, Jill reminded me of the size of the dining area in our tiny house and I reluctantly came to my senses.

We then went downstairs and saw a wicker chair and ottoman that got us both so excited we forgot our pledge not to buy anything that day. We had to have it—even though it would be another year before we'd have a space for it. Francoise, who runs the store, asked us if we could wait until after lunch—it was almost one o'clock and she had to rush home to her apartment to make lunch for her husband. We agreed; it was Rome and nothing is more important than lunch. She told us about a little trattoria right down the street that was hard to find because it had no name, no sign—you just had to know about it. She told us there might be a line but that it was worth the wait. We made a plan to meet her after lunch, we would bring our car over from the hotel and see if we could fit the chair into it.

Lunch was perfect. We were the only non-Romans in the place. There was no menu—just a few pastas and a few *secondi*—very simple, good and cheap. Afterward, we checked out of the hotel in Prati, aimed our car toward the Piazza Navona and plunged into the Roman after-lunch traffic frenzy. The mantra for driving in Rome is "Never look back, never look to the side and above all, never hesitate—just step on the accelerator and pray." There were no parking spaces anywhere near the Piazza Navona; there were no spaces on that entire side of the river. So we crossed back to the other side and found a spot—totally illegal—right in front of the police station next to the Castel St. Angelo. From there we walked across the pedestrian bridge and right up to the Via Governo Vecchio. Francoise was waiting with our chair and ottoman and a young fellow from the barbershop down the street who was all set to carry the chair to our car. We paid her, exchanged phone numbers and promised to be back for more once we had the rest of the house built. Then the three of us wended our way back across the bridge, carrying the chair and ottoman as best we could. We put the backseats down and managed to squeeze the furniture in, completely blocking my rear view—which I wouldn't need anyway because, as I said, if you look anywhere but straight ahead in Rome, you'll never have the courage to move an inch.

We decided to chance leaving the car—filled with our new furniture—for a few minutes longer so that we could race back to the Piazza Navona for a gelato at Tre Scalini. We reasoned that being parked in front of the police station—albeit in a no-parking zone—would discourage thieves.

Jill got the *nocciola*—hazelnut; I got my trusty *straciatella;* and we strolled around the Bellini fountains and then into the side streets. The great thing about Rome is that there's no one "Old Section" where tourists go to see antiquity—it's everywhere, all mixed in with the new. So the city is like a river, in that its past, present and future are all rolling by you at the same time. We felt different about Rome that day—less like tourists and more like we belonged there.

We took off around four-thirty, heading vaguely north. We got lost seven or eight times, and then found our way out of Rome and onto the A1. In an hour and a half we were home. Rome was ours—to play, shop or eat gelato in—as long as we never looked back.

Twenty

THE NEXT WEEK WE KEPT PRETTY MUCH TO ourselves—playing house, lying low. Guests require attention. And if the guest happens to be one of our kids, they require even more. We wanted Alison to be excited by Umbria, to realize that it was a resource for her. We wanted her to meet our friends and get a feeling for the lifestyle, which had meant dinner parties almost every night—either cooking at someone's house or trying one of the restaurants we love. We showed her Trevi, Spoleto, Assisi and Perugia; and then we traipsed all over Rome, walking the cobblestones until our feet were bloody stumps. We were all ready for a break.

Jill and I do an odd thing sometimes—we play down our love for the sake of the children. It's not a conscious choice, but we think, somehow, that if they see how strong we are for each other, they'll feel less love flowing in their direction. So we tame it down a bit. It's not all that obvious; the kids may not even notice it. But eventually it takes a toll on us. When we're less in touch, less demonstrative, and when I don't have Jill in my radar quite as much as I like to, we feel the difference. It's a little embarrassing that we dote on each other so much. It started with the cancer and picked up steam during our time in Marin—all those courses somehow gave us permission to be more intimate—and it's become a habit.

After Alison flew back to L.A., we had a week to find each other again. I cooked every night—just for us. We took long hikes; Jill did some watercolors; I wrote a bit. We casually poked around the area, checking out some towns we hadn't seen yet. Bevagna is a beauty; Montefalco, Spello, Foligno—each one is worth its own six-week visit. So we put a bookmark in them with a promise to get back and give them more time. But this week, the time and attention was for each other.

For better or worse, we cultivate this closeness. The better is obvious, I suppose. The worse is that one of us will die first and the other will be left alone. Some couples we

Lucky guy

know hedge against this eventuality by maintaining a distance, by emphasizing their individuality. But that's not for us. A friend of ours died this year—of a terrible cancer that took him all too quickly. We went to a memorial service at his house and after everyone else had their say, his wife got up. They had been joined at the hip, too—very much in love. She said that once they accepted the inevitable direction of the disease, they would lie in bed every night and hold each other, and they would play this song on the CD player. She put on the song for us to hear. It was Boz Scaggs' version of the old song "For All We Know (We May Never Meet Again)." As Jill and I listened to it, we saw our future as plain as day. We drove home in silence and when we got there, she turned to me.

"Are we crazy? To put everything on each other?"

Crazy? Yes, in that we lose for sure in the end. But I don't see what choice there is at this point.

Caroline's arrival would be easy because she's not a guest. We've lived together in Mill Valley for seven years so we're all quite comfortable with each other. And, as I said before, she always brings lots of energy into the house and a completely new perspective on everything. She challenges every decorating decision we've made; she forces us into a workout schedule that I've managed to get Jill to forget about; she juices things up in general, which is why we love having her around. But Caroline is entering a new phase in her life. She's individuating, as it were. She found a new job; she's cultivating her own friends and her own lifestyle. Cliff and Johanna, who would be arriving shortly after she got here, are her friends, not ours together.

On the other hand, she feels nervous about distancing herself from us. We've become a family of sorts and she's drawn a lot of strength from being a part of the unit. So now she's like a young bird, flying out to test her new powers, then darting back to the nest to make sure there's still a mortadella sandwich waiting for her on the kitchen counter. (Is there a mixed metaphor there?)

I make it sound like we're her parents, which we're most certainly not. But the twenty-year age difference, plus the fact that Jill and I are settled into a long-term commitment, makes us feel very wise—a perfect position from which to give advice, which is probably why she's individuating.

Johanna has known Caroline since they both lived in Jakarta as children. They took hula lessons together. Then they met again years later in Mill Valley and have been close friends ever since. She'd been hired by Cliff to work at a large trade show in Germany, so they were traveling together. Johanna is also very beautiful, and the image of her and Caroline walking and shopping the streets of Umbria—the only Asians for miles around—is an appealing one.

Cliff is a successful businessman whom Caroline met at her gym in Mill Valley. She says he's a friend, but he clearly has other ideas and is in full pursuit of a romantic relationship with her. Cliff is very lavish with his gifts. He buys only the finest things—with the finest labels. And he buys most of them for Caroline. He arrived with Johanna at our humble house in Umbria driving a large BMW, his arms filled with beautifully wrapped boxes: Prada bags, Burberry scarves, Chanel perfume—nothing but the best. Caroline has a whole closet filled with expensive tokens of Cliff's ardor.

He wanted to give us things as well.

"I've been going over the Michelin Guide and I see

there's a two-star not very far from here. I'd like to take you all out to dinner."

Now this was indeed very generous, but I tried to explain that the Michelin Guide is meaningless in Italy. It's totally not the point. Sure, there are some wonderful upscale restaurants and we'll go to one occasionally just to have a change, but the real dining experience in Italy—certainly in Umbria—is the classic trattoria, one that makes simple regional specialties perfectly. To go to a place that tarts up its dishes, gives them a "new spin," adds flavor on flavor until you can't really taste anything, is the opposite of experiencing good Italian food.

"But I insist on taking you to dinner," said Cliff. "And I insist that we go to a really good place. I want to give you a treat."

Something inside me had to burst this bubble for Cliff. Perhaps I didn't like that he was confusing Italy for France; perhaps I didn't like that he wasn't heeding my obviously superior knowledge on the subject of Italian food; or perhaps I was a little jealous—well, territorial—over the fact that Caroline had a new guy in her life. Anyway, I felt I needed to bring him down to earth. I told him I would take care of the reservation, and then I went to the phone and booked a table at Dei Pini in Spoleto.

Dei Pini is the lowest of the low; it is the least pretentious restaurant I have ever been in. The parking lot is an abandoned field; the entrance has those beads hanging down to keep the flies away; the design is classic "railroad," with one room after another all lined up in a row. The chairs are painted red and the walls are covered with posters from old Spoleto Festivals mixed with photos from the good old days. There is no menu and you have to speak fairly good

Italian or you won't get much to eat. It is the opposite of a two-star Michelin restaurant, and it is one of my favorite meals in Umbria. This, I decided, is where Cliff would properly learn to humble himself before the true glory of Italian cuisine.

The first thing we noticed as we passed through the beaded curtain was Giancarlo. He is the boss—the father, uncle and husband—and he has complete control over the entire operation. Not only do his waiters snap to attention when he speaks, but so do—pathetically—the customers. You don't want to be on the wrong side of Giancarlo. He reminds me of an Italian Lou Jacobi—in the way he assumes a lofty disdain for everything and everyone from a face and stature that is anything but lofty. Giancarlo is an everyman, a Chaplin, a big red nose protruding over a push-broom mustache. But he carries himself like an emperor, like a god come to earth.

When we entered the room, I caught Giancarlo's eye. I wanted him to know that we were on time; we would get points for that. I watched him wave—much like a circus ringmaster—to one of his scurrying nephews, who instantly brought bread and water to our table. I noticed Cliff looking around in bewildered amusement at Dei Pini's ambience— or lack thereof.

"I still owe you a dinner," he whispered to me as we took our seats.

Jill, Caroline and Johanna were involved in a very deep discussion—about Italian shoes, I think—when we felt a powerful presence appear at the end of the table.

"*Allora.*"

This is Giancarlo's opening line—every time. It carries many meanings: Stop talking; listen only to me; I won't repeat this. The table quickly quieted down. Giancarlo let a hefty pause fill the space and then he began, in stentorian tones, to proclaim the menu. His eyebrows lifted in bored disdain, his body listed to the left as if he could barely keep himself awake. The words were sung in a slow, measured cadence—not unlike the mourners' kaddish in the synagogue:

"*Antipasto della casa; bruschetta; minestra di farro.*"

"Oh, that's what I'm having," said Caroline about the spelt soup. "I always have that."

Giancarlo cast a baleful glance in her direction. He doesn't like to be interrupted—which makes it very difficult when you have people at the table for whom you need to simultaneously translate. Giancarlo wouldn't last a week at the United Nations. He barreled forward.

"*Strangozzi tartufo; gnocchi con patate; tortellini con panna; tartufi. . . .*"

"That's incredible," I whispered to Johanna. "It's tortellini in cream sauce with truffles and—"

His voice rose over mine.

"*Spaghetti all 'amatriciana; spaghetti carbonara.*"

He then took a slight pause, as usual, to indicate that he'd finished with the first course and was now ready to go on.

"*Secondi: filetto di manzo, tagliate con rucola, faraona. . . .*"

"Oh," said Jill, as if struck on the head with a blackjack, "that is amazing. Guinea hen, grilled until the skin is crisp but the inside is still juicy. . . ."

Giancarlo waited patiently for her to finish. He was quite taken with Jill and suspended all rules when it came to her.

"*Per lei, faraona.*" He smiled at her with a twinkle in his eye.

"*Si,*" purred Jill. "*E un'insalata—invece di primi.*"

"*Ma certo,*" snapped Giancarlo, almost saluting.

Now, what had just happened was that Jill had ordered her whole meal—out of turn—completely interrupting Giancarlo's sacred rhythm. Not only that but she'd asked for salad instead of pasta for her first course—unheard of; and Giancarlo, suddenly as fawning as a lapdog, gave her everything she wanted.

When Giancarlo got ahold of himself again, he sang the rest of the menu—a grilled chicken; tripe; *polpette,* which are meatballs; and *lumache,* which are snails. Then he went around to see what everybody chose—except, of course, for Jill, whose order would be taken care of by him personally.

Three different pastas were ordered, which was great because I would be able to taste everything. Johanna and Caroline asked for half-orders, which is meaningless at Dei Pini. All pastas are served family style and there is always, blessedly, too much.

Then we all told him our choices for the main course— more guinea hen, a grilled chicken, some sliced steak with *rucola.* And then we got to Cliff.

"I'll have the snails," he said. "And I'd like to look at a wine list."

First of all, I didn't realize there was a wine list at Dei Pini. We've always made do with the *vino della casa,* served in pitchers, which—although it's nothing to write home about—goes down quite easily with the food. But, to my surprise, there was a wine list—also oral, not written—and Cliff found himself a very nice bottle of Orvieto. To go with his snails.

Snails? At Dei Pini? Snails were not a local specialty, as far as I knew—although they were ubiquitous as a garden problem. But why wouldn't he order something that we all recommended? Something the restaurant was famous for? Was he doing a *French* thing? *Escargot?* Was he stubbornly trying to have his Michelin two-star meal in spite of me?

The pasta came—and Jill's salad, served personally by Giancarlo. I allowed myself large helpings of the tortellini with truffles in cream sauce, the *spaghetti all'amatriciana,* and the *strangozzi tartufo*—just to get over my frustration with Cliff. He passed on pasta—unbelievable!—and insisted on continually filling my glass with his far superior wine. I allowed him this indulgence only because I was, after all, his host.

His snails came. They looked horrible, buried under a tomato sauce. Bad choice, Cliff! He couldn't get through them, although he gave it a good effort. Later that night— much later—they apparently came back to haunt him. I'm told he was in the *bagno* for the better part of the night and morning. Reading the Michelin Guide, I have no doubt.

Twenty-one

CAROLINE TOOK HER FRIENDS TO PERUGIA, then went with them to Rome for a couple of days before Cliff and Johanna flew back to the States. So, with time to ourselves again, we invited JoJo and Bruce over for dinner. Actually, we had them over because JoJo offered Bruce to help us do some things around the house. Then afterward—if he came through—we promised to feed them.

They arrived at seven so that Bruce could get through his chores while I cooked. He brought his power drill and hung shelves in the kitchen while I chopped fresh porcinis; it was all very creative. Then he followed Jill—drill in hand—to hang pictures on the stone walls of the living room. Then he went to work on our *caldaia,* which wasn't properly heating the water. He took the whole thing apart—the little mechanical bits neatly arranged on the floor next to him—and then slowly put it back together. When he was done, we had perfect hot water. In the meantime, JoJo and Jill were in the kitchen keeping me company.

"I told you, he can do anything," JoJo said. "He ended up

building our entire house out of the pile of rocks we bought. So now he's a plumber, an electrician, a stonemason. . . ."

". . . . Freudian analyst, masseur," called Bruce from the other room. "Disc jockey. . . ."

He'd brought an audiotape with him—a compilation of swing tunes that he had put together over the years. We put it on while I got the fire going in the *camino* for grilling the *secondi*—a mixed grill of pork ribs and sausages. The trick, Bruce gently pointed out to me, is to build the fire against the back wall of the fireplace and then, as the logs break down into coals, move them forward under the grill. That way you can continually feed the fire without changing the intensity of the heat under what you're cooking. Bruce is a master of this technique.

We opened a second bottle of wine while the pasta was cooking. The first had disappeared in a whisper.

Under the pergola with Bruce and Jill

"Tell us about Mexico," said Jill. JoJo and Bruce had taken a two-month vacation in the Yucatán that winter.

"We looked at birds," said JoJo. "And we danced. That was about it."

"Doesn't sound so bad."

"It was too hot to do anything else."

"Have you guys bird-watched before?" asked Jill.

"Nope. First time. Lots of great birds there."

"Did you photograph them?"

"No. I just looked at 'em. Bruce took some pictures, didn't you, honey?"

"At first, but not too much. We didn't really go down there to work."

"How's the food?" I asked. They both shrugged and made a face.

"Nothing to write home about. Some fresh fish comes by in a truck every day. And the tequila's good and cheap. Mexico's not really about the food. Not like Italy."

"Mexico's the music," said Bruce. "There's always something playing—out of a doorway or blasting out of a truck on a loudspeaker. It gets so that you don't even notice it. It's just there in the background—like a sound track."

"Yeah, we managed to dance every day," said JoJo. "That's our goal down there. When we're not watching the birds."

I tasted the pasta, which was just three bubbles away from perfect. The sauce, warm and ready, was bits of sausage, cream and porcini mushrooms—*Pasta alla Norcia,* in celebration of a trip we'd made there the day before. You can find some pretty fantastic sausage in Norcia.

I opened another bottle of wine—Montefalco Rosso, which was fast becoming my favorite. By then it was time

Making pizza dough

to dish out the pasta and pass around the *parmigiano* for grating.

We talked and ate in that way you do in Italy. The time passes gently; there's no sense of hurry or direction. The fire would be ready when I needed it. I dropped another thin log in the back every now and then so that the coals would be hot whenever we finished the pasta course. The rule seems to be that the cook sits with everybody and leisurely partakes of the first course. Then there's a break while he—or she—goes to get the next course together. The idea is to take your time and enjoy the company and not be popping up all the time.

I could tell that Jill really liked these guys by the way she was getting so personal with them so quickly. By the time we got the meat on the table, she was giving them her rap on the Enneagram, which was one of the New Agey things we had picked up in Marin. It differentiates personalities into categories—numbered one through nine—and you have to figure out which number fits you best. The Enneagram comes from an ancient Sufi tradition, I think, and some people study it quite seriously, but we mostly use it as a dinner party game. Jill lists the nine different personality types, doing five minutes or so on each of them, and then our guests try to figure out which number best suits them. By the time everyone's properly identified themselves—with the opinion of their mate thrown in, of course—a kind of psychic strip poker game has taken place.

Bruce is a Seven, like me. Sevens are called *The Epicure.* We epicures love to get a taste of everything—food, locales, sensory and sensual experiences, professions . . . everything. We're a lot of fun to be with. JoJo's an Eight —*The Boss.* We talked about what a good combination they were—with JoJo calling the shots and Bruce, with his vast array of talents and interests, delivering the menu. Jill's a Three—*The Performer.* Which means that she wants everything she does to be the best. Or rather to *appear* to be the best. That's an important difference. Otherwise she'd be a *Perfectionist,* which is a One. Are you following this?

I cracked another Montefalco Rosso, which went very nicely with the ribs and the conversation. Jill brought out a green salad and we lingered, the talk—now that we were all properly numbered—drifting on to our kids. Their son, Miles, would be going off to college the following fall. He was thinking about going back to the States—after spending the last eleven years growing up as an Italian kid. It was going to be a big transition.

"It'll be a transition for us, too," said Bruce.

"And an opportunity," added JoJo. "That's what Mexico is about."

"How'd you choose Mexico?"

"It's cheap. And it's warm; I hate the cold."

"And how 'bout those mosquitoes?" said Bruce. "Can't find anything like them in Italy."

"Well, you'll just get one of those nets and hang it around the bed, right?"

"Right," said Bruce, smiling. He'd give JoJo anything she wanted.

All this talk of Mexico was a little off-putting. Were they really thinking about leaving? For a year? Who would pay my taxes if they were in Mexico? Who would fix my *caldaia*? Who would teach me how to make pizza in my wood-burning oven? Not to mention that they're the most fun people we'd met in years. I was not at all happy at the thought of losing Bruce and JoJo for a year.

"All right, here's an idea," said JoJo, somehow sensing my dip. "We'll crank up the tape and all clean the dishes together. Then after, we'll dance."

We all agreed this was a good idea. Bruce opened a bottle of grappa they'd brought and we all had a little glass before getting up from the table. Then we had a second—except for Jill, who doesn't drink much. She can nurse a single glass of white wine for an entire evening and talk the next day about how she's got to slow down. Bruce turned up the volume of the tape player and the sounds of Kay Kyser and his orchestra bounced off the stone walls of our cottage as we moved into the kitchen to start cleaning up.

The grappa was now flowing like wine. We were harmonizing along to the music, washing and drying the pots and pans and putting everything away where it belonged, and somewhere between "Blue Moon" and "I'd Give a Dollar for a Dime," the fateful second bottle of grappa was opened.

We cleared the floor as best we could in the living room so that there would be room to really swing about. Bruce racked up "In the Mood" and the dancing began.

Jill and I have done quite a bit of dancing over the years. On one anniversary, back in our New York days, Jill surprised me with ballroom dancing lessons, while I had gotten her an evening of dancing at the Rainbow Room at the top of Rockefeller Center—all unbeknownst to each other. It was like our own little O'Henry story. So we know how to Lindy.

Bruce and JoJo, on the other hand, looked to have more zeal than actual practical terpsichorean skill. We could see elbows and knees flying off in all directions and big enthusiastic grins on their faces, but nothing they were doing really resembled dancing. The room was rocking, though.

Then, after Gene Krupa's solo on "Sing, Sing, Sing," Bruce came across the room and grabbed Jill's hand, indicating it was time to change partners. Jill had realized with the opening of the second bottle of grappa that the evening had slipped out of her control, so she shrugged and twirled herself under Bruce's arm, trying to get her steps and Bruce's—and the music—to somehow agree with one another. After a while, though, I noticed that she gave up and was just waving her arms about wildly and bouncing around the floor, following Bruce's energetic lead.

JoJo and I were not doing so well, either. First of all, there was the question of who was leading. Remember, JoJo's an Eight, and what with all the wine and grappa, the Enneagram was screaming at her to take control. I tried following as best I could, but moving backward with my right foot was a very odd way to begin a dance; I couldn't get the hang of it. Not that it mattered—Benny Goodman and JoJo were not in any way marching to the same drummer. But by God she had enthusiasm! At one point—she was coming at me out of a spin at seventy miles an hour, minimum—I frankly didn't know what to do with it. My whole life flashed in front of my eyes. Just standing my ground—or God forbid trying to catch her in some way—would have been to commit suicide. I held out my arms wide, running back and forth like a shepherd, somehow herding her toward the center of the room. We needed space. Help me, Jesus, we needed space.

Later, after the sweat dried, we sat around and recovered. JoJo and Bruce told us stories about their times together and we did the same. We had a lot in common, in that we've changed our skins a number of times over the years; and we've let—nay, encouraged—our partners to change theirs as often as they felt necessary. This seems to me crucial if you want to stay together for a long time. We all value having a "passport" that allows us to cross between the arty, bohemian world and the straight world and be accepted on both sides of the border without too many questions being asked; this is important, because there's too much to miss on either side. This passport thing is big. Sometimes money will afford you one; fame is even better. JoJo and Bruce have neither and yet manage to do brilliantly. This is because they have the most important prerequisites, which are a strong, sure sense of who they are, a heady sense of adventure, and the support of a mate, who— at that crucial moment halfway out on the gangplank when you get weak in the knees and fear you're being a fool— assures you that indeed you are a fool, and that's just fine.

We offered them a room to sleep in.

"No, Bruce can drive; he's very good."

Bruce nodded to me, and I knew it was true. The dancing had sobered him up enough to drive home safely. We hugged them good-bye and sent them on their way. Then we climbed the stairs to our bedroom, feeling fairly exhilarated, as I recall. Maybe we were surprised we still had a night like that in us.

Twenty-two

THE NEXT MORNING DAWNED PAINFULLY and I squeezed my eyes shut, trying not to move my head. The three aspirin I took in the middle of the night were long past being any use to me. It was one of those mornings when you swear off grappa forever. If only the pain would go away—never again. When I came downstairs, Jill was having breakfast outside. I made coffee and joined her.

"Bad night, honey?"

I grumbled back at her. She knew damn well I'd had a bad night. She just wanted to remind me—to underline it. She feels that because I'm a Seven—remember that Enneagram stuff from the last chapter?—my tendency is to forget pain and remember only pleasure. That's why we Sevens tend to overdo on a regular basis—we only recall the fun part. Her goal in life is to help me remember the pain, which on this particular morning was redundant.

Martin had called, she told me, and invited us to take a hike up in the mountains above Pettino, which is a tiny village about fifteen kilometers above us. Jill wanted to go because Martin had told her the wildflowers would still be in bloom at that altitude.

"Now?" I really didn't think I could make it right away.

"No, we're picking up Caroline from the train station at noon, remember?"

This "remember?" had the tone of an accusation. She was pissed at me for drinking so much.

"Of course I remember. Who's Caroline?"

She let go a rueful little laugh and the tension was gone. Thirty-four years together and I can still make her laugh. This could be the whole secret.

"We'll pick up Martin and Karen around three—after lunch—and we'll all go in one car," said Jill. It was a done deal; I was going hiking with a major hangover.

Martin and Karen are another couple with a reckless sense of adventure—as well as a very romantic history. She's a bit older than he is. Well, let me rephrase that—he's a bit younger than she is. They met in Munich, where she was teaching a modern dance class. Martin was taking the class with some other young architects because they thought that learning to dance would somehow inform the way they looked at their architecture—something about bodies moving through space or some such nonsense I never understood. Anyway, here's this German architect stumbling through an American modern dancer's class in Munich, and they took notice of each other. They were both in other relationships and not really available, but the spark was undeniable.

"I asked her to tango," said Martin. "And that was it. The moment I touched her and we began to tango, I knew that my life had changed forever."

Karen had to return to her dance company in Philadelphia; Martin followed and stayed as long as he could. They both shed their other relationships. For a year they carried on a long-distance romance and one day—in a moment of reckless frustration—he proposed to her. They were married in Philadelphia and then continued their bicontinental existence, with Martin's work keeping him in Germany.

He asked her if she would ever consider moving to Europe so that they could be together.

"I told him that I had three more pieces I wanted to create with my company," Karen said. "Then I'd be ready to retire from dance."

So Martin left his architecture firm in Germany and came to the States to be with her. He found a job in Philadelphia and finally moved in to live with his wife.

"I was known as 'Mr. Bamonte' in Philadelphia," he told us, referring to Karen's last name. "She was well-known there and I was the husband. I liked it, actually."

After Karen had finished the work she had committed to do, they looked about for a place they wanted to live. Karen didn't want to settle in Germany, which was fine with Martin. They were both drawn to Italy, where Martin had lived for a time, becoming fluent in the language. A friend suggested Umbria, which they visited, staying at the very same Castello di Poreta that had enthralled us on our first visit. They stayed; Martin found work; Karen plunged into ceramics, which she had studied in college, and eventually turned to sculpture. Her current pieces—stunning heads made of wire mesh that seem to float through space—reflect back on her dance background.

Art is a big connection for these two, as much as the romantic side of things. Martin is an abstract painter as well as an architect; he is also a fine classical pianist. They share a taste for music, painting and theater, although frankly, I find them both a bit weighted toward the dark side. If anything has a light, uplifting theme, a visual image that one might be able to recognize or, God forbid, a happy ending, they're instantly bored with it. It occurred to me that this elevated attitude toward art is one of the things about Martin that gets under JoJo's skin.

Speaking of JoJo, she called just before we left to get Caroline at the train station.

"Are you guys still speaking to us?" she croaked over the phone.

"Of course. Why?"

"Well . . . sometimes the grappa makes us do funny things. We didn't do anything funny, did we?"

I suppressed the image of the Lindy.

"Funny? No, I don't think so. I don't really remember much, to tell you the truth."

"Oh, that's a relief. How 'bout Jill?"

"Jill remembers everything. Want to talk to her?"

She passed, discretion being the better part and all.

We collected Caroline, who seemed very happy to be back in the bosom of her family again. She was adamant about the fact that no one could ever be as exciting, entertaining or just plain fun to be with as us. We agreed and noted that it was nice to have her off with friends every now and then, as she always came back appreciating us all the more.

Because of our hike commitment, we decided to simplify lunch by stopping at one of the *porchetta* stands along the Via Flaminia. As we speak, the powers that be are building an autostrada, or superhighway, that will run north from Spoleto to Assisi and Perugia and take all the tourist and truck traffic off the Flaminia so that the road can return to its more local, rural personality. But for now the big semis roll along it pretty continuously day and night—except for a break at lunchtime, when they pull off to the side and partake of the delectable offerings of the many *porchetta* stands along the route.

The *porchetta* vendors are actually trucks themselves, but all rigged up to be rolling delicatessens. You can get salami (or *salume,* which is kind of the plural of salami) or tuna or sausage—all decked out on a fresh, crusty *panino.* But the star of the show is the *porchetta,* which is an entire pig that has been slow-roasted the night before and carved generously before your eyes onto the *panino,* salted and wrapped in a piece of butcher paper so that half of it is temptingly hanging out the end, then handed to you out of the back of the truck so that you can eat it leaning up against the guardrail while watching the traffic zip by.

A porchetta truck

Making panini

Our favorite *porchetta* truck is usually parked on the west side of the Flaminia just past the entrance to the Tempieto di Clitunno—an ancient Roman temple marking the source of the Clitunno River. Its proprietress is known locally as Miss Tunisia because that's the country from which she hails. But moments after she crossed the border she fixed herself up with a dye job, pierced various parts of her anatomy and, in the Italian style, exposed her belly button for all the world to see. She is a caution, and she knows it. She has a sly, sexy sense of humor and uses it to flirt outrageously with her customers—including me—and she slices a mean pork sandwich in the bargain. No surprise that she has the truckers lined up for kilometers all along the Flaminia.

One thing the drivers stop for—besides the chance to peek down Miss Tunisia's tank top—is a quick shot of *caffe corretto* to help them cope with the morning traffic. This can be literally translated as "corrected coffee"—the correction being a healthy shot of grappa poured into the brew. So keep this in mind the next time you think about swinging out into the passing lane on an Italian highway.

The secret of the *porchetta* sandwich—besides the consummate freshness of the pork—is the crackling that gets doled out meticulously onto each sandwich. Crackling is, of course, crisp-yet-juicy, intensely flavored pieces of pork skin. Yes, we are talking about fat here; I won't deny it. But this is the kind of fat that's very good for you. At least emotionally.

We parked on the other side of the road because the big trucks had cornered all the space both north and south of Miss Tunisia. We patiently waited in line and watched her flirt outrageously, carve meticulously and dole out with a generous hand the grappa that goes into each small cup of the truckers' espresso. When it was finally our turn, she greeted us with the enthusiasm of a long-lost family member and took our order. We watched her carefully pile a good half-pound of fresh-sliced roast pork, laced with crackling, onto each crispy roll, wrap them in paper and hand one out to each of us. She told us to pay her later because she knows you need both hands to handle the sandwich. Then we tucked ourselves in protectively between two huge semis and had the best lunch money can buy. Fast food Italian style.

We picked up Martin and Karen around three and headed up the steep, narrow road toward Pettino, which is a charming but tiny village—small enough to qualify as a *borgo*, except for the fact that it has a quaint trattoria cut into the hillside

Karen

that apparently attracts quite a good crowd on weekends. Martin directed us past Pettino, which sits at 1,000 meters above sea level, up the hill toward Monte Serano, which was where we'd be hiking. Monte Serano reaches 1,429 meters at the summit. I asked Martin if we'd be needing oxygen at this level and he answered me quite seriously that we wouldn't, my attempt at irony sailing right past him.

We parked the car to the side of the road and climbed over a barbed-wire fence, trespassing onto a cultivated field, and started hiking up toward the summit of Monte Serano. It was a serious climb and my thighs rebelled almost immediately. I also had trouble catching my breath, the second bottle of grappa taking its toll on me now. Caroline, of course, leapt ahead with Martin, who looked very professional in his hiking boots and shorts, while Karen hung back generously with Jill and me. We schlepped up the hill for an hour or so, with Martin calling back to us the names of the flowers, which were incredibly beautiful. It was like an endless carpet of color.

"Do you see the orchids?" called Martin, who is an amateur botanist as well as a mountain goat.

And indeed there were orchids everywhere. Yellow, purple and pink orchids, and in between them were blue flowers with tiny petals in the shape of a sphere.

"*Globularia!*" cried Martin from above. "The Latin name for the blue flowers is *globularia!*"

As if I gave a flying fuck what the Latin name was.

We caught up to Martin about twenty minutes later at a particularly steep section, where he and Caroline were staring at something on the ground.

"I am very excited, I must tell you," said Martin, his face flushed with the fervor of discovery.

"*Tulipa sylvestris!* It is a wild tulip that I have never actually seen before except in a book!"

We looked at the flower, which had six pointed petals, yellow inside and brown outside. It looked like a tulip. Mostly, I was thrilled to be able to stop climbing.

"And look at this!" cried Martin, truly enthused. "*Fritillaria!*"

He was now poking around in a shrub, separating the leaves so that we could see a little flower inside.

"In Germany it's called the checkerboard flower. They are extremely rare."

The flower, which was exquisite, had a bell-like shape with beige and purple sections that indeed looked like a checkerboard. Jill and Caroline were cooing over it like girls and asking Martin the names of everything, when Karen— who admitted she wouldn't know a daisy from a gladiola— tapped me on the shoulder and pointed out to the horizon.

We had all been looking down so intently at the flowers that we had forgotten where we were.

Mountain after snowcapped mountain stretched out as far as we could see, making our little Monte Serano seem like just a bump. And dominating them all was Monte Vettore which, at 2,476 meters, was the highest peak in the Sibilini chain. Directly in front of us, framed by the mountains, was a small incline that led down to a flat meadow, filled with flowers.

"Oh God," said Jill, "I've always wanted to do this."

She stretched her arms out and ran down the hill to the meadow, and as she reached the bottom, she whirled around and around and starting singing, in her exquisite lyric soprano, "The hills are alive with the sound of music. . . ."

Julie Andrews, eat your heart out.

Twenty-three

THE DAY BEFORE WE LEFT we met with Martin, JoJo, Nicola our contractor and Sophie, who would be doing the landscaping when all the construction was finished. We sat under the pergola, went over the budget and looked at the little Rustico for the last time. Nicola had brought some samples of *pianelle* for us to choose from. *Pianelle* are brick tiles that are the traditional flooring in Umbria. He showed us a brand-new one, then a new one made in the old manner so that it looked antique and, finally, a real antique. There was no question what we wanted—the antique tile had rich red and ocher running through it that simply couldn't be duplicated. He said he thought he could find enough to at least do the new entranceway and *salotto*.

The next day, big earthmoving machines, cement mixers and power saws to cut the stones would move in for the better part of a year, and when they were done the house would be doubled in size.

"It'll be World War Three here when you come back in September," said JoJo.

"We will seal the two connecting spaces with heavy plastic," said Martin, "so you will be able to live in the old part while we're building the new. But there will be noise. And dust."

This was actually helpful. It gave us a motivation to leave. Otherwise there was little reason for us to go back to Mill Valley. We felt like we'd be missing everything. We hadn't spent a summer here yet—only spring and fall. In a few weeks the Spoleto Festival would begin, filling the little town with dancers, musicians, actors and the tourists who would come to watch them. We would miss that. Then Umbria Jazz would start up in Perugia for two weeks. It was fast becoming one of the great jazz festivals in Europe. We'd miss that. The *Infiorata* in Spello was only a week away. Each year—on the feast of Corpus Christi—the eight thousand or so people who live in this beautiful medieval town decorate the streets with lavish "paintings" made of the petals of flowers. Then, in a day, it's gone. We would miss that.

And we'd miss our friends. On the Feast of San Lorenzo, otherwise known as the Night of the Shooting Stars, Bruce and JoJo, Martin and Karen, Bruno and Mayes, Sophie and Jeff, George and Mariane would all camp out in the Pian Grande and watch the meteor showers. Bruce would barbecue; George would bring the Prosecco. Oh God, would I miss that.

It's not that we didn't have things to go back to—Jill needed to visit her mom in Santa Barbara; we wanted to try to get our acting careers out of mothballs. We had things to do. It was just that Mill Valley—for all its natural beauty and creature comforts—wasn't the right place to do any of them.

· · ·

Sophie

The day we left Campello it was pouring. We got up at 5 a.m. in order to drive the two hours to Fiumicino and catch a 9:45 flight back to the States. Caroline had a flight on another airline leaving about forty-five minutes after ours. I knew we'd hit traffic, so I left the appropriate amount of leeway to make sure we would get there in time. The car leasing company had a deal where it would meet us at the departures curb and take the car, so that would help.

We sleepily carted our suitcases through the rain and heaved them into the back of the car, locked the doors and the heavy wooden shutters of the house and silently said good-bye. Well, not completely silently. As we drove away in the dark, you could hear sleepy, sad voices counting off the treasures.

"Good-bye, olive trees." That was Jill.

"Good-bye, little house." Me.
"Good-bye, mortadella." Caroline.

We hit the Gran Raccordo Annulare at full morning rush
hour and came to a dead stop. The GRA is a highway that
makes an enormous circle around Rome, and it's the only
way I know to get to the airport. At 7 a.m. we patted ourselves on the back for having left a sizable cushion; at 8, after having moved perhaps five hundred meters, we vowed
never to do it this way again—we'd come in the night before, get rid of the car and stay at the airport Hilton. At
8:30 Jill and I kissed our flight good-bye and concentrated
on getting Caroline to hers. And still the traffic crawled. Jill
used our cell phone to try to contact both the airline and the
car rental company, but had no luck.

"First, there's that damn recording of that woman
telling me there's no such number. Then I call again and
get through—to the airline's answering machine. I guess
they're not open yet."

"Italians," I mutter. "They're having coffee."

"That poor car rental guy has been standing out in the
rain for almost an hour."

"Can you get through to the company?"

"That same lady telling me there's no such number."

"That's bullshit; I got through on that number yesterday."

"*Italia.*"

We fumed and inched our way toward Fiumicino.

Then at around 9 the traffic magically evaporated and we
found ourselves speeding at eighty miles an hour, holding the
merest wisp of a hope of catching our plane. We'd have to

get rid of the car, check four large suitcases and clear security—all in the thirty-five minutes before the plane would push back from the gate. Given that the airline asks you to be there two hours before, our hopes were not high.

We pulled up to the curb and our car guy, drenched to the bone, was waving us down. I barked at Jill to sprint for the airline desk—to let them know we were coming; Caroline would help me with the luggage. I gave Jill the wallet with the tickets and passports and she moved off through the crowd.

I signed the contract for the car, quickly detailing the various scrapes and dents that inevitably come with parking in Spoleto, and hauled the luggage out of the back. Caroline, in the meantime, had secured a luggage cart. When we got inside the terminal, we had to join a long line to clear security just to get to the airline desks. This was in addition to the regular security after check-in. There were the standard armed soldiers in camouflage who were demanding we show our passports to get through—the passports I had thoughtfully given to Jill. It was now 9:15.

"Mike, catch!"

This was Jill flipping the passports to me over the head of the security guard.

"They're trying to get us on but you've got to get through this line!"

I thought about how I was going to explain this to the Italian soldier blocking my way with an Uzi draped over his shoulder. I decided to just wait my turn.

We arrived at the airline ticket desk at 9:25. Caroline helped us get the luggage off the cart and then waved good-bye as she ran to catch her plane. I turned to the woman behind the counter, who was looking grimly at our luggage.

"I am very concerned that you will not make this flight," she said. "It is very late for the bags."

"What can we do?"

"Follow me."

And with this, she hoisted the largest suitcase up onto her hip and headed through the crowd toward security. We grabbed the rest of the bags and followed. She cut us into the front of the line and helped us to lift the bags up onto the X-ray machine. Meanwhile our guardian angel was smoothing things over with another Uzi-armed soldier and with some airport security personnel—and also with the people we had cut in front of in the line.

"I am sorry, but we have to inspect the inside of this bag."

This was a very stern-looking security woman who seemed to be well connected to the guy with the gun.

"There is a large metal object. . . ."

I realized that she was concerned about the five-liter can of extra virgin olive oil that I had packed carefully between my socks and underwear.

"Oh, that's olive oil."

"*Scusi?*" said the Uzi.

"*Olio,*" I translated.

"*Da dove?* He was suddenly very interested. He wanted to know where the oil came from.

"*Trevi. Da un frantoio locale.* Extra virgin. This last phrase needed no translation, as it's become adopted as an Italian phrase, very much like "al dente" has become American. I explained as best I could in my broken Italian that this *frantoio* still used the cold process of extracting the oil.

"That's difficult to find these days," he said in Italian. "You must be very careful where you buy or you could end up getting Spanish oil." He said these last two words as if he had said "cancer."

He started to unscrew the top to have a little taste—just for security reasons, of course—when Jill blurted out, "Leave it, we've got to go!"

And four jaws simultaneously dropped open in disbelief— our airline lady's, the security lady's, the soldier's and mine.

"Leave it? You want to leave *this* olive oil?" the security lady said in disbelief, her finger shiny with a taste of oil on it.

The soldier with the gun licked his finger again and threw a scornful look at Jill. He was thinking perhaps that he might have to waste her. Our airline lady saved the moment—and Jill's life, maybe—by quickly explaining, in Italian, our dire situation.

They nodded and handled the can of oil like a religious relic as they tucked it back into its nest. We still had to get a shuttle train that would take us to the departure gate. It was 9:38—the plane pulled back in seven minutes. We shook the hands of all the security people, with whom at this point we felt a bond, and went for the train, our airline lady clearing the way for us like a downfield blocker. We still had all the luggage.

We bolted off the train and headed down an escalator, following our lady, who was still carrying the heaviest bag: she wouldn't let me take it from her. Then we hand-carried the luggage into the plane and gave it to the stewards, who in turn handed it through a special door to the luggage handlers. We'd made it.

Our airline lady was flushed with excitement. I grabbed her and hugged her with all the enthusiasm of the moment. Then Jill hugged her very emotionally and we both started to thank her as best we could in Italian. She looked at me very intently.

"You are Italian." It was a statement.

"No, American."

"But I mean your parents. . . ."

"Actually, no. Lithuanian Jewish."

She beamed at me like a headlight.

"Before I die, I move to Israel. And become Jew."

Jill and I stared at her, nodding, not knowing quite what to say.

"I move to Israel. And become Jew. Before I die."

We continued to nod and say that it was incredible. We were witnessing a religious conversion and—even though the stewards were in a hurry to close the plane door—we didn't want to rush her through it. After a proper pause, we hugged her again and then waved her all the way down the exit ramp.

We would miss Italy.

Twenty-four

WE RETURNED IN SEPTEMBER TO CONSTRUCTION chaos. A gaping hole had been dug for the pool; septic line trenches snaked their way through the former orderliness of the olive grove as if a gigantic gopher had run amok. There were ugly piles of building supplies—broken concrete block, unused rocks, wooden pallets that had held the roof tiles—and, dominating the front yard, a construction trailer and strips of bright orange-red plastic tape acting as a fence to keep us out of the danger area.

On the good side, the roof was on the new addition and the stones were being cut and secured into the walls. There's a tradition: "*Tetto sulla casa; pasta alla piatta,*" which means, "When the roof goes on the house, you owe the workers a pasta dinner." We talked to Nicola, our contractor, and decided to schedule the dinner after Caroline arrived a week or so later.

They were building in the old style—so that the walls of the addition would be as thick as those on the old Rustico, providing the same quality of natural insulation. The house was framed in concrete block, not wood. Then, on the outside, stones were set in stucco to form a second layer, and the inside was covered in several coats of plaster. So the walls are two and a half feet thick—a veritable brick shithouse. Nicola showed me how he had chosen local stones that had the right color and feel for this part of Umbria. I asked him if he thought he could visually match the new addition to the old house.

"*Sará uguale?*" I asked him. Will it be the same?

He looked at the old house for a long time, smiled and said, "*Meglio.*" Better.

It was true—the old house had been built centuries ago by very poor people. They used whatever they had—rocks, bricks, mud and then, later, cement to patch up cracks caused by the many earthquakes in the area. Looking up close, it was a three-and-a-half-century hodgepodge of building materials—but from ten feet away, it looked like the picture-perfect stone cottage you've always dreamed of. A little ivy crawling up a wall helps a lot.

The addition, however, was being built with beautifully matched rocks—all at least eight inches in girth—and a stucco (pronounced "stooko") that had been subtly colored with ground-up stone from the local hills. Enzo, Nicola's brother, called Jill and me out one day to help choose the color for the stucco. Enzo is brother number two.

"This is the one Nicola and Martin have chosen," he said, pointing to one batch of tinted mortar, "but you have to make the choice. You are the owners."

Damn straight.

"But be careful. The color becomes darker when it dries."

Jill asked if we could do test areas on the actual wall,

then wait until they dry to make the choice. Enzo thought this was a great idea and mixed two other batches—one lighter in color, one with more of the reddish dust. We picked a wall on the back of the house where our test strips wouldn't show so much, and Enzo applied the three different stuccos between the rocks with his mason's trowel. A mason in Italian is called a *muratore,* and Enzo is a master.

"*In tre giorni, vedremo*—we will see," he said.

As we got closer to study the different tints of mortar, Enzo suddenly stopped and took Jill's arm.

"*Guarda!*" he said, and pointed to the sky.

The clouds had thinned and shafts of sunlight were streaking through the orange and purple sky onto the hills of shimmering olive trees—like in a painting by some Renaissance master. Better. We stopped in our tracks and stared. We were quiet for a long time.

"*Bella, no?*" he whispered. "*Bella Italia.*"

"Yes." We nodded. Very bella, indeed.

The next day we were talking with Ivano, brother number three. Ivano is the youngest, the only bachelor of the family and quite a nice-looking fellow.

"Nicola is the smart brother. He is the one with brains. Enzo is *caporeparto,* the foreman."

"And you?" we asked.

"*Schiavo,*" he said with a big grin. The slave.

The three brothers come from Naples. They are here in the north because there's not enough work to sustain their families in the south. Nicola and his wife, who is a teacher of special education, have moved here permanently and just had their first baby. Ivano decided to follow his older brother to see what life was like in the north, and Enzo, whose wife and kids are still living in Naples, commutes back home every weekend. The three brothers have a close family tie, which, in Italy, is redundant.

"*Vi piace la bandiera?*" Ivano was asking if we liked the flag that was flying high over the new roof.

We said that we were very happy with it. Martin had e-mailed about a month earlier, saying that there's another tradition—of raising a flag once a new roof is completed. He told us that the workers didn't think it made all that much sense to use an Italian flag and asked if we wanted to raise the American flag. We nixed that idea because the U.S. had just invaded Iraq and we weren't feeling very identified with our country.

"Nicola asked if you would like the peace flag," e-mailed Martin.

We thought that was a great idea, and so did all the workers. It's still flying over the house.

We noticed that Vittoria, our cleaning lady, would bring out a thermos of hot coffee for the workers at around four in the afternoon. They really appreciated it, so Jill and I started to do it as well. The first time we had only three takers because it was during Ramadan and our workers from Tunisia were not allowing themselves any stimulants. One day I brewed a pot of American coffee—just to see how everybody liked it. Ivano sipped it and said, unenthusiastically, "*É buono—ma non é caffe.*" It's okay, but let's not pretend it's coffee.

Vittoria came once a week—to clean, to bring us fresh eggs from her chickens and to brighten our day. She has an extraordinary vitality that perks us up every time she comes. Vittoria was born and raised in the neighborhood, but—because she had spent her working years in the employ of the Agnelli family, of Fiat fame—she had traveled all over the world and lived, for the most part, in Rome until she retired. Now she cleans for us because she's loved the Rustico since she was a little girl and loves to spend time here. Which makes us very lucky.

"Domenico wants to speak with you. About the olives. He'll come later today—*dopo pranzo.*" After lunch.

Domenico—nephew to Vittoria, husband to Laura, who owns the fresh pasta shop—is retired from his job as foreman of a large plant in Terni. He's still a young man (well, younger than me), and he's agreed to take care of our garden and grounds. At the moment, he is in a waiting mode while the construction crew rips up the site, but—along with Sophie, our landscaper—he's been making plans for when the house is completed.

Later that afternoon, the five of us (Vittoria stayed around to supervise) walked around the construction site, imagining how our garden would be situated the following summer when everything was done. We decided to have a separate herb garden just outside the kitchen, along the east wall of the *forno*. The vegetable garden would be down below the pergola—near where the parking area is now. We'll have tomatoes, eggplant, peppers—both hot and sweet—zucchini, beans, lettuces and *rucola*. Since we were changing the entrance and parking area to the other side of the house, the old parking area would become the site of our *bocce* court. No Italian villa is complete without a *campo di bocce*. Then Domenico suggested that he plant artichokes all along the perimeter fence below the *bocce* court. They would take a couple of years to develop, but eventually we would have our own *carciofi*—and enough for all our friends—every spring. Then Domenico made his proposal about the olives.

"Since you are leaving in the middle of October, you

will miss the olive harvest, which takes place from the end of October to the middle of November. So, I propose to harvest all the olives for you, take them down to the local *frantoio* and then put your very own oil into five-liter cans, which will be waiting here for you when you return. You should have at least thirty liters, maybe more."

Vittoria beamed. She had obviously been in on this plan.

And I'm thinking the perfect rejoinder to this incredible act of generosity would be the old Hollywood line, "Oh yeah? What's in it for me?" But they wouldn't have gotten it.

The dance between Martin and JoJo continued throughout the building process—although we experienced most of it by e-mail. This didn't really bother us because they seemed to be competing for the job of who would protect us better. At one point they were in deep disagreement over the moving of the electric gate and finally decided to confer with us—the clients—about our opinion. Martin assumed we wanted the electric gate at the new entrance for a number of reasons—security, privacy and convenience, to name a few. JoJo hated the electric gate and thought Martin was being obsessive.

". . . as to the electric gate, here's my concept" her e-mail read. "You get another gate, a pretty gate—*senza elettricità* (without electricity)—not necessarily immediately— and when you arrive, say in September, you open the gate—and when you leave, say in October, you close the gate. If you leave for a couple of nights in Roma, you close the gate when you leave and open it when you get back.

"Soooo, instead of having to open and close the gate every single fucking time for every person who comes and goes which, by the way, does nothing to protect you since, if it's broken which, by the way, happens continuously, people just have to climb over the little fence next to it to get in—you'd just leave the pretty new gate open. *Capito?* (understand?) I say get rid of that massive hunk of junk with its dreadful flashing lights, so you don't have to worry about who has the clicker and if the clicker's batteries are working and if there's a thunderstorm, has it shorted out and stopped working and will the olive grove neighbor be calling and cursing our name? etc. etc. etc. Do you sense how much I hate that huge, ugly piece of shit?"

Martin just sighed—if you can sigh in an e-mail—suggesting we do what we want—and not be swayed by any "outside influences." He agreed that Italians, historically, were overly concerned with walling themselves in and that a closed gate didn't offer us any actual security. In general, he was in agreement with JoJo about the gate, and his only problem was that he didn't want to appear like he was in agreement with JoJo.

Vittoria took us on a little walk around the property to show us the bounty of wild herbs and greens that grew under our feet and along the roadside. We had noticed local women (and occasionally men) dotted along the shoulder of the road—some with baskets, some just stuffing their pockets—gathering greens for dinner.

Cicoria—wild chicory—is everywhere. Vittoria pointed it out and we collected a fair amount of it. We also picked some wild oregano, which she said would make a good *tisane*—herbal tea—that was especially good for colds and sore throats.

Back in the kitchen, we washed the *cicoria* to get the dirt and sand off and then dropped it in boiling water until it was tender. This is crucial to get rid of its bitterness. Then Vittoria demonstrated how to drain it and sauté it in garlic and olive oil. She told us we could add some white beans at this point and have a classic *cicoria e fagioli*—greens and beans—or make a chicken soup with *cicoria,* pecorino cheese and a scrambled egg or two floating in it, like *straciatella* soup. *Cicoria* was a staple at this time of year and all we had to do was walk out into the front yard and pick it.

That night, we met all the regulars at the Palazzaccio to catch up on the gossip. When we came through the door, Danila greeted us with a big hug and we fell into conversation with her before we joined the crowd at "expat table." We'd noticed that we'd been speaking nothing but Italian for the last few days—to Nicola, Enzo and Ivano; to Vittoria and Domenico—and we were able to communicate with Danila on a higher level than before. We still weren't discussing literature or anything like that, but the knot of tension in the back of my neck—which I got whenever I entered into an Italian discussion—was considerably smaller. We realized that we actually *preferred* to speak Italian. Walking around the property with Vittoria, arguing with Ivano about American and Italian politics, wading through Domenico's strong Umbrian dialect to finally discover the meaning of his words and the generosity of his heart—we started to realize that the only way to know Italians was to speak Italian.

So we decided to plunge in more deeply. My birthday was coming up in February—my sixtieth. Jill had wanted to throw a party with friends from all the different parts of our lives congregating in Umbria. But February wouldn't be a good time to do that. So we decided to put the party off un-

Home

til summer and celebrate my birthday by enrolling in a language intensive for two weeks in Rome, studying Italian all morning and playing in Rome the rest of the day and evening. Then we'd come home to Campello on the weekends to be with our friends. We'd also never been in Umbria in the winter, and the locals had been telling us it's really the best time—quiet and cozy, and the winter truffles are far superior to the summer ones. I e-mailed our travel agent and booked a three-week trip in February and called and enrolled us in the language school in Rome.

Twenty-five

WE STARTED FISHING AROUND the expat community for the real story on JoJo and Bruce's Mexico plans. Were they looking to spend a few months of the winter down there? Or were they actually thinking about transplanting themselves—and the party that always surrounds them—down to the Yucatán Peninsula? It was hard to think about losing them so soon after having found them.

Sophie was over to check on the three almond trees behind the house. They were being seriously threatened by the construction and she wanted to make sure they would survive. After she reassured us that at least two of the three trees would make it, we asked her what she knew about Bruce and JoJo's plans.

She was quiet for a while, which made me think there was a secret she didn't want us to know. Then she shook her head.

"I'm not sure. I think they're telling people a little bit at a time, so that nobody panics. You know, JoJo's made herself completely indispensable to a lot of people here. She has a secret weapon: Bruce. He can fix anything, cook anything, build anything, find anything. And with her managing skills, they offer an unbeatable service."

It was true; we depended on them a lot. JoJo paid our bills and taxes; she was the liaison between us and all the Italian tradespeople. She knew the intricate workings of the Italian bureaucracy and how to maneuver through it. Both she and Bruce translated the culture for us as well; they knew where the best *sagras*—festivals—were, the hidden treasures, the best food sources. Bruce was my mentor with the wood-burning oven, my grill-master.

"But you don't need them for any of that, do you?" I asked Sophie. She and Jeffrey and their son, Elias, had been living here for thirteen years and spoke Italian perfectly.

"No. We'll just miss them. They're our best friends."

A couple days later, we got a call from JoJo, inviting us over for dinner. Bruce was doing his famous lasagna and they said they needed some good eaters. She acted as master of ceremonies in the kitchen as we watched Bruce do his thing.

"Yeah, he's good with all that flour stuff. He can make anything."

JoJo waved her hand vaguely toward Bruce, who flashed his Cheshire cat smile and blushed. He was feeding fresh-made pasta through an old hand-crank machine that was bolted to the edge of the kitchen table, kneading and smoothing it. We had just watched him make the dough from scratch in no more time than it took us to walk across the room. He had mounded some "0" flour on the table, created a little well in the middle and put three very fresh eggs into it. Then he took a fork and deftly combined the flour into the egg until he had a ball of bright yellow dough with a satiny texture that just begged to be touched.

"If the oven works, this could turn out to be a pretty good lasagna."

"Yeah," added JoJo. "We got this oven from Mariane and George when they did their kitchen over and it's a little dicey. It sort of cuts out when you try to heat it up."

"Other than that, a perfect oven."

JoJo poured red wine for everybody from a magnum-sized refillable bottle. It was a Primitivo they had bought in jugs on a trip down to Puglia the weekend before, and it was definitely a cut above the usual *vino della casa*. Even Jill, who wasn't much of a red wine drinker, held her glass out for more.

"It works very well as a doorstop," JoJo said.

"Or a very big paperweight," added Bruce.

"Sucks as an oven, though."

Bruce was tightening the rollers on the pasta machine, and with each pass the sheets got thinner and thinner. When they were almost transparent, he dropped them in the boiling salted water, one at a time, and when each was done—in seconds—he transferred them to a waiting bowl of cold water.

"I have an oven method that I think is almost foolproof," he said.

"Didn't work last time."

His little smile again.

"Yes, but now I've perfected it."

He took a large stainless steel spoon, opened the oven door and clanged the spoon three or four times against the heating element in the bottom of the oven. Then he lit the flame, holding in the dial for a few minutes. It looked to me like he had succeeded.

"Now let it go," said JoJo, grimly.

He did, and the flame went out and the kitchen filled up with the smell of propane. Undaunted, he tried his method a few more times: banging it with the spoon, holding in the dial, releasing it—and filling the kitchen with gas. On the fifth try, the oven stayed lit.

"Now, here's the important part."

He used the same spoon to prop open the oven door—just a few inches.

"Or it just goes out again."

The sheets of pasta, now all partially cooked, were drying on towels. JoJo daubed at them gently with another dish towel to make sure they were completely dry. The two of them worked the kitchen nicely together, anticipating each other without ever making a show of it.

"Can we do anything?" I asked. "You're doing the work and I'm drinking all the wine."

"You're doing a very good job," said JoJo.

Bruce handed me a big chunk of nicely aged *parmigiano* and the microplane grater we had given them the last time we were here. We'd given one to Bruno and Mayes as well. And to Martin and Karen. It was perhaps the only real improvement we could offer the Italian kitchen.

"How much?" I asked.

"About half a cup."

Not very much, I thought, for a whole lasagna.

Bruce ladled out a small amount of tomato sauce—with a metal spoon very much like the one stuck in the oven door—onto the bottom of a ceramic lasagna dish. Onto this he gently placed a few sheets of pasta, making the first layer. Then he spooned on some béchamel.

"At least we *have* an oven," said JoJo. "The two months

we were in Mexico last winter, the house didn't have one. Nothing at all. We did all our cooking out on the barbecue."

Here it comes. Mexico.

"So . . . what's the plan?" asked Jill, in a voice a little higher than the situation called for.

Bruce glanced at JoJo, and she shrugged. Over the béchamel layer, Bruce spooned some more tomato sauce, and over that he sprinkled the lightest dusting of *parmigiano* with his fingers.

"It depends on whether we can rent this house."

"And what we can get for it. The idea is to have the rent we get for this place cover all our expenses for a whole year down there," said Bruce.

"And that's it—a year!" blurted JoJo. "Then we'll be back."

This time she poured the wine just for herself.

"It's not like we're leaving Umbria. One year, that's it."

That made me really nervous. Why did she have to say it twice? Were they really thinking of leaving forever? They had just sent Miles, their one and only child, off to college in New York and were feeling that desolate kind of freedom that Jill and I went through when Max went off, never really to return. And Bruce was sick of his job. He had been teaching English to the Italian Army for the past ten years and he'd just got word that they were cutting back on the program. So he was about to make less money for a job that held no interest for him anymore.

In a funny way, I wanted them to go. They're the trailblazers, the role models for starting new chapters, for keeping your life and your marriage energized and exciting. I didn't want to think of them as being stuck here just because wimps like us didn't think we could live without them. The truth is we would never really take a full bite of Italy as long as they were here to catch us each time we slipped. Once they're off to Mexico, we'll *have* to learn Italian, I thought; we'll *have* to make the culture our own; we'll *have* to learn how to get inside.

"Taste this," Bruce said, holding out a spoon to me. It was the freshest, most delicate of all tomato sauces.

"How'd you do this?" I asked.

Fresh tomatoes from the garden, carrot, celery, onion. A little salt. Don't sauté anything; just let them bubble up together in a pot. Maybe a little sugar. Then puree it.

"It's from Marcella's book," said JoJo. "She's still the best."

The amazing thing about the sauce was its softness. There was none of the acidity that you usually find with tomatoes, just a round, subtle softness.

Bruce made three or four more layers of the lasagna—the thin strips of pasta, the béchamel, the tomato sauce dusted with *parmigiano*. He carefully moved the stainless steel spoon aside, opened the oven and placed the lasagna inside. Then he expertly lodged the spoon back in place and rested the oven door against it. He had indeed perfected the method.

We cracked another bottle of the Primitivo and sat down in front of the fireplace in the dining room. As we waited for the lasagna to become itself in the oven, Bruce put a marinated butterflied pork loin on the grill over the fire, where he could watch its progress from the table.

He brought in the lasagna and carved perfect squares for each of us. I tasted it, and it filled me with an odd sense of longing. Then I took the next bite and realized that's what I had been longing for. Why was this the best lasagna I had ever eaten? Ever dreamed of eating? Because its texture was like a fragrant, silky pillow that disappeared almost before I could fully enjoy it? Because its taste was a subtle blending of flavors so close to one another—eggy dough, sweet, soft tomato, nutty *parmigiano,* buttery béchamel; a pastiche of pastels, not vibrant oils? Because it teased my senses, flamed my desire, stirred the greedy, gluttonous beast that lies, licking it chops, just below the surface of my cheery, unimposing exterior? Or was it just that I knew—as I inhaled my second serving—that I would have to travel all the way to the fucking Yucatán if I ever wanted to taste it again?

Twenty-six

THE MAIN PIAZZA IN OUR LITTLE TOWN—the only piazza, actually—is not a postcard-worthy town square the likes of Trevi, Bevagna or Montefalco. Our town is not on the tourist trail. It's strictly for the locals, and I must say I prefer it that way. There are three bars, two butchers, two *alimentari,* a fruit and vegetable shop and a number of various other retailers—but if you didn't know they were there, you wouldn't be able to find any of them. We lived there a year and a half before we knew that the doorway next to the church—the one with the beads hanging down to keep the flies out—was Gloria's *orta-frutta* shop, the best and freshest local produce in the area. There's no sign, nothing. If Karen hadn't told us about it, we'd still be walking right past it without a clue. But once you know about it, you know. The same with Ugo's. There's no ad in the paper telling you that he makes the best prosciutto in the world. You just have to know.

The church on the piazza is a beauty—*Chiesa della Madonna della Bianca,* constructed in the sixteenth century

Our local bar

and looking every bit her age. Her name translates literally as the Church of the Madonna of the White Woman—named after some memorable blond from way-back-when who did something miraculous, no doubt. The church is still very much in use, and we can hear her bells ringing all the way up the valley at the Rustico.

There's a little park across from the church with playground equipment, a statue commemorating the war dead and, most significantly, benches fronting the square with some great-looking old guys who smile and wave to you when you pass by. If a postcard company wanted to feature our village on one of its cards, the old guys—*i vecchi*—are definitely the most photogenic shot in town.

Jill and I were strolling around the square, getting smiled at by the old guys, when we saw a poster on the bulletin board next to the statue in the park. It advertised a drawing and painting class just starting up that would meet every Thursday afternoon at the local music school.

"You gonna do it?" I asked her.

She smiled as if to say that I was joking.

"No, really," I urged. "Why not?" It wasn't that strange a suggestion—she had studied years before at the Art Students League in New York and returned to painting whenever her acting career slowed down.

"I don't. . . ."

"What?"

"A lot of things. I don't speak Italian well enough; I won't be here for the whole course—I'd miss the last two months of it; and I'm not comfortable enough yet with . . . with being a foreigner here and not knowing anybody, really."

"That's why."

Her look changed. I saw the hesitant Jill recede—the one who didn't want to enter any situation unless she was head and shoulders the best in the room—and be replaced by the adventurous Jill, Jill the Conqueror, who would take on any new challenge and suck all the perfection out of it until she *was* the best in the room.

"What do I do?"

"The *comune*'s right over there I think."

The municipal building is on the other side of Gloria's from the church. It's the same building—with a colonnade along the front—that houses one of the town's no-name bars. We asked the guy in the bar where the office was and he told us it was on the second floor. The entire municipal government building consists of two offices and a desk, so it didn't take us long to find what we were looking for. A very nice lady gave us the info and told us that Jill had to pay for the course by buying some special stamps at the post office. At least that's what we thought she said. Our Italian was good enough to get most of it, but not all.

We went to the post office, but the door was closed because it was almost time for lunch. We had arrived at a ticklish time. If you walk into a shop—or even worse, a government office—at ten minutes to one, the people behind the counter get visibly nervous. Because if you want something that may be complicated to attend to—like if you have to try something on or ask a difficult question in fractured Italian—it might mean that they will be late getting to lunch. This is as low a thing as can happen to Italians; it can ruin a whole day. They will often protect themselves by locking their door at a quarter to one pretending they don't hear anybody knocking. Then, at one, they open the door, look at you with feigned surprise and go to lunch, which is way more important than business—especially at the post office, where it's not their business anyway.

It took Jill four days to figure out how to pay for the class, what she needed to bring and where exactly the music school was. And by Thursday afternoon, she was quivering with excitement. I offered to drive her down and pick her up three hours later so that she didn't have to stress about parking and everything. She was like one of our kids on the first day of school.

When I picked her up, she was late coming out of class, so I waited in the car. Ten minutes later she came out the door, calling "*Ciao*" and "*Buona sera*" over and over. Her face was flushed and her eyes were lit up—my favorite look— and I knew we had a hit on our hands. We went out to dinner at La Trattoria, a Slow-Food restaurant we like a lot down on the Flaminia, and she debriefed me about her afternoon.

"Oh my God, it was sixteen local housewives . . . and me. And the teacher said she could speak English, but you couldn't prove it today. Not a word. Not one blessed word. But it was great. These women! They never shut up the whole three hours—yakeda, yakeda—I tried just to focus on the drawing, but it wasn't easy."

"Did you talk to anybody?"

"Oh yeah, on the breaks; I talked to everybody. They were wonderful. I found out who's having a baby, who's going in to have a procedure at the clinic next week, whose husband is putting on weight. Next time I'll drive myself. There's plenty of parking."

So every Thursday Jill collected her art material and went off to class. And every day in between, she would practice, setting up her easel on the table under the pergola and painting away for hours at a time. Sometimes she would just draw. She was reading that book about drawing from the right side of the brain—or the left side . . . whatever. She'd draw a piece of fruit, or her own left hand, which she elegantly posed for herself on the table—over and over until her brain learned to switch off the rational side and function completely from the intuitive side. Over and over and over. Because that's the way she is.

And paintings started to come home with her. Wonderful paintings that she did in class. Her teacher, whose name was Altavilla, was a stickler for technique and each week she taught them another trick—for shading, for perspective, for color. And Jill would work on that one aspect for the week until she got it.

I went down to the *alimentari* one morning to get some

things for breakfast, and Sabrina, who owns the place with her husband and her family, asked me how Jill was doing.

"Are you in the class with her?" I had no idea. Sabrina had never seemed to me to be the artistic type.

"*Si si. Lei é molta brava!*"

And she made a gesture that implied how impressed she was with Jill's artwork—both hands palm up, in front of her chest, the tips of the fingers coming together, and shaking them simultaneously like she was rolling dice.

Up until then, it hadn't been easy for us to break through socially with our neighbors—which is why we hung out with the expats all the time, the Anglophones. It's not that the locals were standoffish; they're actually quite warm and welcoming—especially if you give their language a try. And it's not that we didn't want to get to know them. But our Italian wasn't good enough for us to relax with them, make a joke, be ourselves. We were working on it; we had a wonderful teacher back in Mill Valley and we worked with Paola sometimes in Umbria—although she was now pregnant with twins and it was hard to get her to focus. We had high hopes for the language intensive in Rome in February, and we managed to practice with our construction workers and Vittoria and Domenico, but social situations were different.

We had gone to a party at Bruno and Mayes' house where there were mostly Italians. Even the few expats in attendance spoke only Italian that night. People had to speak slowly to us, with hand gestures, or repeat themselves, or find another, more elementary way of saying whatever it was they were trying to say. Eventually, they gave up and went off to find an adult conversation; I didn't blame them—we were boring.

The frustrating thing was that they were obviously really interesting, attractive, entertaining people, these friends of Bruno and Mayes'. They were artists, entrepreneurs, architects, musicians, great storytellers and personalities—and they were all there for the taking if we could just *parle* a little bit more of the *Italiano*.

I tended to speak out more than Jill, because I didn't care whether I did it correctly or not. When I didn't know a word, I'd often as not just say the English word and put an Italian ending on it—as in "I think I need another *drinkarino*." It was fairly offensive, but I made myself understood; I got through. Jill was appalled by this and tended to wait to speak until she could express herself perfectly, with just the right verb tense, with all the proper syntax. Which meant she almost never spoke. She was, essentially, mute. But always correct.

Also, I had more give-and-take with the locals because I shopped for all the food, did the errands. The problem with this was that the shopkeepers inevitably used me as an opportunity to practice their English, which was even worse than my Italian. Talk about inane conversations. But I also got the opportunity to talk to the people behind me in line, who, for some reason, never spoke any English. So, again, more chance for me to practice.

A couple of weeks after the art class started, we were crossing the piazza when we heard a shout from a little shop that sells lingerie across from the church on the other side of the square.

"*Gille! Gille!*" (Sounds like "Jeelay!")

"*Ciao*, Mariana!" shouted back Jill like a real Italian.

"*Come va,* Gille?"

They were at the top of their voices.

"*Bene, bene, tu?*"

"*Beh.*"

This is my favorite Italian expression. It's a very short word, not strung out like "bey," but quick and punched up with a little rising inflection: "*Beh.*" It means anything and everything. In this instance, it would be translated as, "Nothing's changed; my life is the same old shit; but I'd be a fool to complain about it." It's usually matched with a gesture; you can pick from a long list. Mariana, in this case, held out both hands in front of her with the palms open and facing slightly upward—sort of like a desperate plea for God's help.

The girls both laughed loudly and waved to each other. I was standing there—unnoticed, unintroduced—taking it all in.

"*A giovedi.*"

"*Si, a giovedi!*"

They were saying they'd see each other on Thursday. Jill's pace picked up as she crossed the piazza, smiling and waving to the guys on the bench.

"Where are we going?" she asked. "Ugo's?"

I nodded and tried to keep up with her. But I could tell from her body language that she was feeling good. She had broken through. She owned this fucking town.

Twenty-seven

THE FOLLOWING WEEK WE DROVE DOWN TO ROME to pick up Caroline, who—like the last time—had completed a triathlon just the day before. We felt like the finish line. We welcomed her with the now traditional mortadella sandwich to counteract her jet lag and lift her mood. There was an awkward moment between us when she first came through customs, I think because Jill and I were spending more time away from Caroline than with her—this after seven years of being pretty much joined at the hip. She was coming to Italy for shorter and shorter visits each time— just as our stays were getting longer. She said that she didn't want to spend time in the construction chaos—which was true—and that she was busy back in California with her work and her triathlons—also true—but it was clear that her life and ours were developing different priorities. Our little orphan was spreading her wings; it was good.

I don't think she would have come at all were it not for the fact that her dad was coming down from Switzerland for a visit, and it really wouldn't have worked for her not to be there to host him. Caroline's dad, Kurt, is a world traveler, gourmand and raconteur extraordinaire, so he would be fun to have around. We booked him at a hotel near us because— until we finished construction—we had no room at the inn, so to speak.

We also got a call from our friend Judith Auberjonois, who was in Switzerland with her husband, Rene, visiting his family. Rene, unfortunately, had to get back to L.A. for work, but Judith decided she could accept our invitation to come down and check out our new place. She ended up at the same hotel as Caroline's dad and was great about squiring him back and forth to all the activities.

It was shaping up to be a perfect time to finally fire up the *forno* for a pizza party. I called Bruce and he was game, so we planned it for the following weekend.

We ending up making pizza for eighteen of our nearest and dearest. We figured if we were going to the trouble of firing up the oven, we might as well feed as many people as we could find plates for. Bruce was the master *pizzaiolo,* and I stood behind him and learned some things.

We started the day before, making the dough. Bruce decided to do a little taste testing, so we made some dough from "00" flour, some from "0," some with whole wheat flour mixed in and some with a combination of "0" and "00." These designations of Italian flour indicate how finely ground it is and how much germ and bran have been removed. The "0" is used mostly for bread and pasta, "00" more for pastry. Then we labeled each one and put them in the fridge to rise overnight. I made a tomato sauce from the San Marzanos that were left in the garden and roasted a few heads of garlic in olive oil. We shopped for the mozzarella, sausages, *rucola,* basil, anchovies, olives, potatoes and rosemary, pears and Gorgonzola—all the toppings we needed to make the pizzas to the various tastes of our friends.

On Sunday, Bruce and JoJo showed up around one, we all had a little lunch to tide ourselves over and then Bruce and I went out to start the fire while JoJo organized Jill and Caroline, making the toppings in the kitchen. Bruce had brought along all the tools of the trade from his oven at home: pizza peels, two wooden and one long stainless steel; a long-handled iron rod with a curved prong on the end—almost like a hockey stick—which proved invaluable for moving the burning logs around; and an old bamboo window shade—rolled up—that served as the basic kindling.

He crumpled up some newspaper—quite a bit of it—and made a big, messy pile of it in the middle of the oven. On top of that he randomly threw the smallest sticks we had, and on top of that the bamboo window shade. Then he piled larger sticks—about two inches in diameter—on top of the bamboo, until he had quite a large pyre built up. Then he lit the paper and we watched as the fire fairly filled the center of the oven, which was a beautiful, vaulted chamber made of four-hundred-year-old bricks.

Without much pause, Bruce kept throwing in more wood, slowly extending the fire to the rear and to the sides while feeding the center as well. He just kept tossing in more wood and then used his hockey stick to move it around and make sure there was always enough air between things to feed the flames. My first mental note was that I had been way too timid in terms of the amount of wood I piled on when making fires. This was the beginning of a real inferno.

"When it really gets going, the flames slow down—almost like slow motion. That's when you know it's really getting hot," he told me.

He kept widening out the fire, adding wood to the rear and to the sides, until the fire was five or six feet in diameter. The idea was to get it hot enough so that all the vaulted bricks turned white: then it would be ready for pizza. Bruce estimated that it would get to about 800 or 900 degrees.

The guests were due around three, so I went into the kitchen and punched the dough down and kneaded it for the last time. It felt perfect—smooth and satiny, slightly springy to the touch. And it smelled like I hope heaven will smell. We'd start with a couple of pizzas made with the "00" flour, which Bruce said would be a bit less glutenous. Meanwhile, he was spreading out the fire so that it completely encircled the center of the oven—all except for the opening at the oven door. The pizzas would get intense heat from all sides at once. The flames had slowed down now, which meant we had achieved the intense heat we needed. Watching them dance and lick the ceiling of the oven in super slow motion was the eeriest, most surreal of sights. I went into the kitchen and pulled Jill and Caroline out to see it. We stood there in front of the flames, not quite believing what we were watching.

As people showed up, the corks started popping out of the wine bottles and a little keg of good German beer was tapped—compliments of Sal and Rosemary, a couple we had just met through Bruno and Mayes. They live in Connecticut mostly, but just finished renovating a beautiful old church in Trevi that they get to four or five times a year.

Bruce asked me if we had an old rag or dish towel that we could part with. I found him one and he told me to get it dripping wet and not to wring it out at all. Then he attached it to the end of his hockey stick and swabbed the bricks on the center of the oven floor. Steam filled the oven for a second or two.

"Ready for number one!" he told me.

With great excitement, I ran into the kitchen and grabbed the first ball of dough. I flattened it with the heel of my hand and stretched it out. Then I picked it up by the rim and turned it slowly, letting gravity stretch it out even more. I flipped it up in the air a few times, just to show off (actually, if you do it right, spinning it in the air serves to centrifugally send some dough out to the edge to make a natural rim). Then I sprinkled a tiny bit of cornmeal on the wooden peel—to keep the dough from sticking—and laid out the first, thin circle. I covered it with a bit of tomato sauce, broke some mozzarella onto it—not too much; toppings have to be light —and made a Margherita, the classic pizza named after a queen of Italy (the basil, which completes the three colors of the Italian flag, is added after the pizza comes out of the oven). Then I carried it out and handed the peel to Bruce, who demonstrated the gentle, shuffleboard flick that deposited our treasure right in the middle of the oven.

The pizza responded immediately—almost violently— puffing up and blistering in the intense heat. Bruce, now using the long metal peel, artfully turned the pizza so that it cooked evenly. In seconds—no more than a half a minute—he declared it done. He gently insinuated the peel underneath it and withdrew it from the heat. Then he put it onto a metal pizza pan and told me to start making the next one, which would be a marinara—tomato sauce, no cheese, some roasted garlic and anchovies.

Everybody started to get into the act, slicing up the finished pizzas, flattening dough for the next one, choosing the toppings, eating. Everybody was eating. It became a frenzy. I carried out slices for Bruce and kept his wineglass full. He

Bruce as our pizzaiolo

said that the *pizzaiolo* never leaves his oven until the last pizza is done.

Everyone, of course, had an opinion as to which crust was the best. For me, the combination of "0" and "00" was the clear winner. Bruce thought so, too, and said that the perfect crust should be two-thirds "0" and one-third "00." But his taste (and mine) runs to a more Napolitano crust—a little chewy, crunchy and slightly charred in parts. Bruno, of course, prefers a Roman crust, which is thinner and a bit more like a cracker. Best pizza? Bruce's again—paper-thin slices of potato, topped with olive oil and fresh rosemary. When it hit the heat, the potato crisped up in an instant in the rosemary-infused oil.

We made pizza for five hours or so. The party was half in-side, half out. It was an autumn day and it rained a little here and there, but nobody minded. The oven is sheltered—like a

Bruno, Bruce, and me at the forno

little house—so that the *pizzaiolo* and his trusty assistants don't get wet. We finished up with the whole-wheat crust. We put a combination of pears and Gorgonzola cheese on it—sort of a dessert pizza. After that, Jill and Caroline brought out salad, but no one could eat any more. We had pigged out to the max. That's when the serious drinking started.

A few hours later—the sun had long since set—a few people brought chairs into the sheltered area in front of the oven door and sat around it like it was a hearth, which, of course, it is. I pulled a chair up and joined them, and within minutes there were ten or twelve of us packed in there, talking, drinking, swapping stories, warming our bodies and hearts with the glow of the oven. I felt a huge release inside my chest. It had been a long day—a long two days; and I realized that I had been carrying a lot of tension, anxiety even, about this oven, this *forno a legno*. The day we first saw the house, the oven grabbed my attention. I craved it. When we went back to the States, I longed for it. I couldn't get it out of my mind. Sure, I wanted the little cottage, the Rustico; the land and olive trees; the view. It was all desirable. But the oven was the prize, the real motivating factor in buying the house, moving to Italy and changing our lives forever. That's a lot of pressure to put on an old pile of stones. What if it didn't work? What if there was a hole in it or something? What if it wasn't really ancient but had been thrown together from an old Sears catalog?

It's a beautiful oven. It's been standing on this spot since the early 1600s—long before there was a house—and was the community oven, where the local peasant women (dressed in wimples, no doubt) came to bake bread for the week. It's quite large. It fed, I'm sure, a lot of peasants. It looks like a little stone house, sheltered by an oak tree, only steps away from our kitchen door, just on the other side of the vine-covered pergola that shades our outdoor table. Sitting there in the dark, with all those wonderful people crowded in around me, I peered into the glowing oven chamber to really get a look at it. The vaulted bricks were still white; it seemed so amazingly large, commodious; some medieval peasant family could have all curled up and been quite comfortable in there.

Later, the diehards—JoJo and Bruce, of course; Martin and Karen; Bruno and Mayes; Jill and I; Judith and Caroline's dad—gathered in the kitchen and started singing. We went through swing songs from the thirties and forties and old camp songs; Kurt sang some Swiss-German ditties, and a translation of "Chattanooga Choo Choo" that brought the house down; JoJo did her version of "You Made Me Love You," which was very fetching; and then she and Bruce sang a parody of "La Donne E Mobile" called "La Scale Mobile"—about the escalator in Perugia.

After the singing, we got into a major political discussion. We were down to the *real* diehards at this point. I don't know what the hell we were arguing about—I think everybody was pretty much on the same side of things—when Martin said something, I don't remember what, and JoJo ripped into him about the Germans and the French, who had turned a blind eye to genocide at their very front door, in the Balkans, and they were off. I think these two just like to yell at each other.

The next morning, on my way to the *alimentari* for yogurt and bread, I put my hand on the oven door. It was still warm.

Twenty-eight

WE CAME BACK TO MILL VALLEY a week or so before the 2004 presidential election. Flagrant Democrats that we are, we flew home to make our vote count against the war in Iraq and the administration in general. When it turned out that more than half the country went the other way, supporting the powers that be, we were caught totally off balance. How could we be so completely, diametrically, passionately disassociated from half the population of our country? We read about people—other disheartened liberals— threatening to leave, to go to Canada or Mexico, and we thought about our house in Italy and that we already had a place to go if our feeling of alienation got any more intense. Not that Silvio Berlusconi's government was a model of integrity and righteousness; whenever he was indicted—which was fairly regularly—he'd pass a law that decriminalized whatever crime he'd just committed. But I didn't feel responsible for his government—just ours.

A month or so later, we took a trip to New York to meet an agent and a manager, both of whom had been recommended to us by our old friend and former publicist Judy Katz. The meeting was to be a mutual sniffing out, in that we had to convince them they wanted to represent actors who lived three thousand miles from the next audition. But we met with all concerned, did the obligatory lunches and agreed to go into business with each other on a trial basis. We severed ties with our former agent and now had all our representation coming out of New York.

Back in Mill Valley, we saw an article about an Italian film festival in San Francisco, and that Lina Wertmuller was to be honored on opening night. It had been twenty-seven years since we had worked with her in Rome, and we decided to wangle ourselves an invitation.

The event, an elegant cocktail party before the screening of her newest film, was staged at the Italian Embassy in San Francisco. When we arrived we saw Lina—her friend/interpreter by her side—surrounded by an adoring throng in the middle of the room. We inched our way closer and listened to her respond—in pretty much the only English she could speak—to the compliments coming her way.

"Thank you so much; that's very kind of you; it's so nice to be here in my favorite city in America."

I leaned over and whispered in her ear.

"*Lina, ti ricorda da me?* Micky; Micky Tucker."

She turned with a confused look on her face and stared at me. Then her jaw dropped.

"*No. Non é possible!*"

And then she laughed her wonderful, gravelly bark of a laugh and embraced me tightly.

"Micky! Micky! I don't believe!"

Then she saw Jill and beamed. She embraced her, too.

"*Cosi bella!* Still so beautiful, my darling."

The rest of the evening we were hers. She wouldn't let go of us. Literally. We made a dinner date for the following night.

At dinner we tried to speak only in Italian, which went pretty well until I couldn't find the word for something and tried to talk around it with other words I couldn't find, at which point Lina put her hand on my arm, looked at me with a tired expression and said, "Micky, Micky; spikka English."

She told us she had a friend, an actors' agent in Rome. When we returned in February, she would get us together with her. She thought there was a good chance we could work over there. This brought a whole new aspect into play; the axis of New York/Rome/Umbria danced in our imaginations while beautiful Mill Valley receded, no longer making much sense to us at all.

Then a week or two before we left in February for the birthday trip to Rome, Jill got a call from our new agent. There was an "inquiry" from the Manhattan Theatre Club in New York about a new play they were doing in March—was Jill interested? Yes, Jill was very interested. The play was being directed by Joey Tillinger, an old friend who also happens to have a house in Umbria, whom we visited our last time there. He had mentioned the play and that he was still looking to cast the woman's role, which piqued Jill's interest. She privately asked JoJo to serve as her agent and prod Joey to consider her for the part. These are the kind of confluences that Jill thrives on. The "universe" was telling her that this was the direction her life was about to travel and, as always, Jill put a lot of stock in what the universe had to say. But by the time we were ready to leave for Rome, the voice of the universe had obviously gone off to talk to somebody else and our agent and manager both said they didn't think it was going to happen. So we wrote the play off as a possibility; this kind of thing happens all the time in our business.

Caroline helped us pack—as always. She can artfully arrange a suitcase so that it reaches its full capacity, fitting in at least 50 percent more crap than we would ever get in there. The only problem being that the moment I open it—to get a toothbrush or something—I somehow disarrange the design and can't fit half the things back in.

Caroline helped lug the suitcases to the waiting taxi and we said good-bye to her and the dogs. We told her that we'd call her when we got to Rome and that she should have a great time while we were gone and that we'd see her in three weeks with our Italian much improved. Jill and I got in the cab and waved as it pulled away, not knowing that we were leaving our Mill Valley house for the last time, never again to live in it, nor with Caroline.

First we flew to Zurich, where we'd found a guy who sold good used cars at decent prices; we had negotiated the deal by e-mail. It was another commitment to living more in Italy—rental cars are very expensive in Europe, and having our own car was an investment in our future. We picked up our brand-new three-year-old VW Golf, drove down through the Alps, went around Milano and stopped for one night in Modena, the home of the real balsamica and some of the best food in Italy. That night I ordered fettucini Bolognese, Bologna being only a few miles up the road, and realized that what makes this one of the world's great dishes is not so much the eponymous meat sauce—which was superb, by the way—but the pasta itself. Freshly made before our eyes, rolled out and cut by the hand of a woman who had been making fresh pasta since before she could walk, the fettucini was the star of the dish. The sauce was carefully spooned over as a complement, a support to the pasta, not slathered on top as is done in the States, drowning its subtle flavor and texture in a sea of tomatoey goop. I was feeling very anti-America at that point—that belligerent country, arrogant and myopic, and it oversauced its pasta.

It was wonderful to drive up to our house and see the improvements that had been made since we left in September, although construction had now ground to a halt because of the freezing temperatures. Martin assured us, however, that they would be finished on schedule—and in time for the birthday party when we arrived back in June. Sophie swore that if the landscaping was not perfect and the *bocce* court not finished, I could roast her in the oven along with the suckling pig that we had planned for the party. I got this in writing.

Two nights later we were on the train to Rome. We checked into our hotel and sped off to Maccheroni, a wonderful trattoria just a stone's throw from the Piazza Navona, and then walked the streets, digesting, appreciating Rome in the winter, when it was filled with Romans and not too much more.

At eight the next morning, I went around the corner to a bustling bar filled with people on their way to work. I waited my turn at the counter and then ordered a *cappuccino caffè dopio,* which became my eye-opener for every morning of the intensive. It's the well-known frothy, delicious cappuccino but with a double shot of espresso. I sipped it while I scanned the front page of *La Repubblica,* my favorite lefty/Commie Italian newspaper, and I realized as I circled words to look up in my dictionary that I didn't really know much Italian at all. I took a toasted ham and cheese sandwich back to Jill, who was doing her yoga and meditation in our chilly hotel room (the heat was on the night we checked in, then never again). We took a collective deep breath, put on our winter coats and trundled off to our first day of school.

First thing, we had to take a placement test—to see which level we'd be put into. I have never been good at tests. Well, I've never been very good at school in general. So I gave the test a quick once-over, figured I knew pretty much all this stuff, finished it in five minutes and handed it in. Jill took the full forty-five minutes they had allotted.

Then they called us in individually to see what our conversation skills were. I engaged the instructor in what I thought was a very interesting and charming discussion and she told me my verbal skills were better than my written test results. She told me to go off to room number four, where I would join a class that was already in progress.

I wanted to wait for Jill to make sure we got into the same class. I was sure I spoke Italian much better than she did and I didn't want her to have to enter into a room full of strangers by herself. But she was nowhere to be seen, so off I went to room number four. I opened the door carefully and peeked in. The room was packed, and I took a seat way in the back so as not to interrupt the lesson.

The teacher was talking—much too quickly, I thought— about the difference between the imperfect tense—the *imperfetto*—and the past tense—the *passatto prossimo*. She was rattling on about when you used one and when you used the other and I had no idea what she was talking about. Then she started around the class, asking each of us to solve an example in the book. The girl next to me was kind enough to share her book, since I didn't have one yet. She showed me where we were—at machine gun speed—and when it was my turn, I noticed that my shirt was soaked in sweat. I stammered a few *mi scusas* and *mi dispiaces,* treading water like a son of a bitch, trying to figure out what was going on. The teacher cut me off—a little rudely, I thought—and told me to go down to the office and buy a book: level four. By the time I got back they were onto the *congiuntivo,* which I couldn't even explain to you in English. At that point I kind of blacked out, which happens to me at moments of extreme tension. I was finding it hard to believe that I was putting myself through this torture voluntarily—on my birthday, no less. It was like having my fingernails ripped out.

At the break, I found Jill. She shrugged and said she was finding the whole thing too easy. And I damn near decked her right there in the hallway. Too easy? My God. Then she looked at me strangely and asked if I was all right and I told her that I wasn't and we set off together to the office to find out what the hell was going on. The woman listened to both our stories and then looked at our test results, which she had in front of her—one in each hand. The she smiled and crossed her hands, one over the other, indicating that she had mistakenly sent us to each other's class assignments. We all got a jolly little laugh out of this—never mind that at least ten years had been shaved off the end of my life—and she asked what we wanted to do. Jill told her that her class, level one, would be much too easy—even for me—and I assured her that level four would be much too hard for Jill. Even she didn't know the *congiuntivo.* So we decided to both go into level two, which we certainly knew some of, use it as a little refresher and then learn some things we didn't know. And we'd be together, which is what this was all supposed to be about anyway. And level two turned out to be just *bravissimo*.

We had two teachers—one for grammar and one for conversation. The conversation guy—Franco—was worth the price of admission alone. He was a handsome, strapping fellow, rode a motor scooter to work through the streets of Rome and flirted outrageously with all the young girls in class. And he openly berated anyone who was too shy or afraid to speak out in Italian. He was brutal; he would just turn away and ignore you, as if you weren't there. There were two or three students who transferred out of his class because they felt they couldn't learn from him. But he turned out to be great for Jill. For a day or two she sat there, frozen in fear, and then—because Franco refused to pay attention to her—she blurted. All the syntax was wrong; her tenses were flying all over the place; her endings were askew—but she plunged in. And that was the moment Jill really started speaking Italian. I knew it was right because she sounded a lot like me—completely grammatically incorrect, spouting like a sperm whale. Franco loved it. He went on to tell us that it could take ten years of daily study to get the grammar just right and that most Italians' grammar is horrendous anyway. The point was to speak and let the grammar catch up when it could.

We decided that we would speak only Italian for the whole two weeks in Rome, which led to conversations filled with long pauses as we frantically thumbed through our dictionary in order to finish our thoughts. The Rotunnos had us up to dinner a couple of times, and they promised to also speak only in Italian as well—a much easier task for them. I must admit our language skills improved remarkably—even though my head felt like the inside of a golf ball, with all

those tight little rubber bands wound around each other under four thousand pounds of pressure.

We had dinner with a woman named Pam, whom we
had just met in Umbria. Pam is a charter member of the expat community there, and the only reason we hadn't met
her before was that she was starting her life all over again as
well—in New York. She's actually one of the people who
created the Castello di Poreta, or rather *transformed* it, into
the wonderful hotel where we stayed during our first days in
Umbria. Pam is an American who has lived in Italy for many
years—at first in Trastevere. So she gave us a personal walking tour, pointing to this apartment building and that *alimentari,* spinning for us her romantic story of love and marriage
to an Italian composer and their eventual divorce. The tour
ended at Da Augusto, a tiny trattoria filled only with locals—
not Romans, but Trasteverini. It's such a local place that a
tourist could pass it a thousand times and never know it's
there. Again, we spoke only Italian. Well, mostly.

We met Joie, Judith Auberjonois' friend, a writer who
also lives in Trastevere. She took us to Spirito di Vino, a
more upscale restaurant on the other side of Trastevere—
the Santa Cecilia side—and we ate the best dinner we've
had yet in Rome.

We went—just the two of us—to Baffetto, the great
pizzeria on the Via Governo Vecchio, near our school. I think
it was on that night that we decided—quite unconsciously—
that Rome was really ours. Sitting next to us—the tables at
Baffetto are quite close together—were two young tourists
from Ireland traveling on the backpack circuit. They were
trying out their Italian with the waiter, and not having much
success. It was either anchovies or artichokes they wanted on
their pizza, and the waiter didn't want to get it wrong. After

I'd leaned over and deftly straightened out the whole situation, they looked at me with great appreciation. Well, no problem, Rome's my beat. And I'm bilingual, by the way. Over there's where I got my haircut; there's where we bought our dining room table; there's a wine bar around the corner where they have this great cheese drizzled with balsamica. Check it out.

On the way home, Rome was showing off its winter aspect; it was cold and rainy, dark and shimmering, ancient and vital. We walked through the puddled streets to our hotel room, snuggled under the covers and drilled each other—in Italian, I mean.

The next night the phone rang and our agent said they were offering the play to Jill. She would start the following week in New York, three days after our final class. Jill was conflicted at first; she was scheduled to visit her mother in Santa Barbara—the trip was all planned, and she didn't want to let her mom down. Lora, her mom, was eighty-seven and her husband, Ralph, was ninety, and Jill's visits were very much looked forward to. Jill was also concerned about Caroline and the dogs and her acupuncture appointments in Mill Valley, and . . . I gently reminded her that maybe flying off to New York to star in a wonderful play, just after finishing a two-week Italian intensive in Rome, was not too shabby a scenario for an aging ingénue. She exhaled and smiled, and that was that.

Twenty-nine

WE ARRIVED AT JFK AT FIVE IN THE AFTERNOON, right along with a picture-perfect late winter snowstorm. Jill's contract provided us with an apartment, which, after a little shopping around, ended up being located on the Upper West Side, our old neighborhood. It was a three-floor walk-up in an old brownstone with an utterly useless kitchen, a tiny one-person bathroom and a bedroom so small that we had to get in and out of bed on the same side. It wasn't all that dissimilar to our first apartment in New York when we were thirty-five years younger—shabby, tight as a sardine can and utterly romantic; we were in the first act of *La Bohème* and nobody had a cough yet.

A few days later Caroline flew in like the Red Cross bearing suitcases filled with winter clothes, hats, boots, vitamins, supplements, Chinese herbs and an inflatable bed—for guests (not that we were planning on doing a lot of entertaining). Imagine for a moment how small that apartment was with the three of us in it.

Cristo's Gates were still up in Central Park and we

trekked for miles, wandering along the orange daisy chain that stood out shamelessly against the bright white snow in the park. New York was never this much fun in the old days.

Jill started rehearsal, Caroline went back home and I had the days free to wander the streets, write in my little garret for a few hours a day, shop at Fairway and, when I couldn't put it off any longer, contact my agents to look for work. Mostly, I reconnected with old friends. David and Susan Liederman, who still hadn't completely gotten over the fact that we left New York twenty years before, were delighted to have us back. They now had a restaurant farther upstate in Mount Kisco and were well-connected—as always—with the food scene in New York.

Whenever Liederman came into town for business, we'd tie up for lunch, hunting through Chelsea or the meat-packing district or Chinatown for great, cheap food. It was as if I had never left. And Susan, who has been the somme-lier for all their restaurants over the years, added me to the list of the Susan Wine Club—which every couple of weeks delivers a handpicked case of fabulous, little-known wines at scandalously low prices. Being on Susan's list is reason to move to New York all on its own.

We fell in again with Ron Shechtman and Lynne Meadow (Lynne runs the theater where Jill was performing). Between them and the Liedermans we had invitations to get out of the city—to Connecticut or Westchester—whenever Jill had a day off.

At voice-over auditions, I reconnected with old buddies from our early days in New York—all older but not in any way wiser. One afternoon I ran into Chris Murney on the Upper West Side and we sat on a bench in the middle of

Broadway, sipping coffee, cars whizzing by on both sides, and reminisced like the two old geezers we had become.

Jill was deep into her work. And I enjoyed welcoming her with a hot meal when she got home. If this had happened (and it did) in our early years, I would have felt jealous and peevish, but now—Thanks to what? Growing older, being together as long as we have, all the courses we took in Marin, or maybe the success I'd managed to achieve on my own?—I was free of any obligation to compete and just enjoyed being there for her. I even let her fall in love with her costar—just a little.

We invited Lora to come and visit when the play opened. This way we could circumvent any guilt Jill may have felt about not visiting her mom. The idea was to let Jill have her experience—unadulterated—without having obligation to anyone or anything else. And it worked. About three weeks into the process, she came home lit up like a Christmas tree.

"This is what we should be doing, honey. Plays in New York!"

I had no argument. The idea of splitting our time between New York and Italy seemed to me to be a perfect life. When the work dries up, which it always does, we'll hop over to Umbria and fire up the pizza oven. It was all I could do not to pick up the phone, call my real- estate broker in Mill Valley and put the house on the market. But I remembered that the flush of excitement you have in the third week of rehearsal could be seriously eroded on opening night, when the critics come and bring everyone back down to earth. We decided to wait until the play opened before seriously considering uprooting ourselves. If Jill still wanted to move after that, we'd get into it.

I did, however, start to prowl around the neighborhood, checking out open houses on Sunday afternoons—just to get the lay of the land. In my mind, I wanted to find an apartment that cost about what we'd get for our house in Mill Valley—just a little flip job. But when I looked at a dozen or so in that price range, I became frustrated. I called David Liederman, who is as shameless a real estate slut as I am, and told him my problem.

"I can't find anything in that price range that I wouldn't be embarrassed to bring my friends to."

"Forget it," he said flatly. "Not at that price. But I have a tip for you."

"What's that?"

"Call it a pied-à-terre. Then all your friends will love it. They'll say, 'Ooh, what a wonderful pied-à-terre!' You'll have a shitty apartment, but a great pied-à-terre."

In the middle of all this tumult, another change occurred that took us completely by surprise—around the third week of March, spring happened. We had forgotten what spring was like when you have to wait through the whole, long winter. Spring in California comes too easy. And it's so close to the experience of winter you're never really sure it's happened. That ain't it. Spring is when the earth defrosts after months in the freezer and gives off an aroma that's as good as pizza dough rising. It's when the scrawny branches outside the window of our garret are—overnight—filled with green buds all the way down the block. It's walking through Central Park with thousands and thousands of other people who are as happy as you are to be able to open your coat and feel the sun on your skin. Spring is orgiastic. Jill walked every day to rehearsal and back, through the park and out onto Central Park South, and I think she enjoyed that as much as the rehearsals. Spring was about change, and so were we.

The play opened and Jill received love letters from the critics. They essentially agreed with what she'd said in the third week of rehearsal—that New York is where she should be and plays are what she should be doing. That was it. The gloves were off—we were moving to New York.

I called Caroline with the news, which we knew was not going to please her. Her home was being sold out from under her and her adopted family was abandoning her for New York. Even though she had been moving on her own in the direction of independence, to have it be our decision was a lot tougher to take. And we'd be asking her to adopt our dog, Buddy, as well. Buddy was twelve years old and set in his ways. He thinks there's too much traffic in Mill Valley, so we all felt New York would be too much of a shock to his system. Caroline also agreed that Buddy and Jade, her dog, should not be separated after all those years together.

But Caroline's a survivor extraordinaire; she always has been. She found a great place to live, renting Birgit's guest house—Birgit, whose birthday party in Puglia was the start of our whole Italian adventure. She can keep both dogs there and walk them on the same trails they're used to. She'll have her job, her friends, her triathlons—everything except Mike and Jill to come home to.

It was a big change for us as well. We would be living "two in a box" for the first time in thirty years. Our kids were both up and out, pursuing their own lives, and now Caroline would be doing the same. We would have to see what it was like to have only each other as roommates after all these years.

Jill's mom's visit was a triumph. We put her up in a furnished apartment just down the block from us. It was an apartment usually rented out to visiting opera singers at the Met. Lora thought that was just perfect. She had her privacy, her own kitchen and bath, and yet we were steps away if she needed us. She went to see Jill's play, of course, which she loved. We had given her the script beforehand because her hearing's not so great anymore. This way, she had no trouble following the plot. We decided to give her the full New York experience: galleries, shows, concerts, lunch at the boathouse in Central Park—the whole schmear. Lora got a good four-month cycle out of the trip—a month of excited planning, the trip itself and then at least two months of bragging about it to her friends and neighbors back in Santa Barbara. She had been worried she wouldn't be up for a trip like this, but the moment she hit the Big Apple she seemed to shed fifty years. We planned immediately to do another trip the following year.

I did a guest shot on *Law and Order,* which was fun. I did a few play readings. I hunted up voice-overs. And I planned my belated sixtieth birthday party in Umbria—Mike's Birthday Observed. The party was originally set for the middle of June but when we got to New York the theater told us they wanted an option to extend the play until the first of July. This would not work for the party, so I canceled it. But a number of people—the Liedermans, my brother Ed and his wife, Barb, and others already had their plans booked and were coming anyway. So when it turned out that the play wasn't extended, we went forward with a scaled-down version of the party. Scaled-down in guests, that is—not food.

Liederman, who had already threatened to do a pig in our oven, now also wanted to roast a baby lamb. He asked if I had a good butcher. A good butcher? I had four. David said he expected the party to last a week.

We found an apartment—a lovely two-bedroom pied-à-terre only six blocks from where we lived in the old days. Our Mill Valley house sold before we put it on the market. We made plans—with Caroline's help and supervision—to move most of the furniture and all the art across the country, where it would be stored until we got back from Italy. Then we'd move in and start our new life.

Thirty

WE ARRIVED BACK IN UMBRIA and plunged almost immediately into a vortex of festivity. On Sunday night, Mariane and George threw a farewell party for Bruce and JoJo at Due Querce (Two Oaks), a trattoria/pizzeria near where they live. They bought out the entire patio area and had about fifty of their friends to a sumptuous feast. This was the kickoff to a series of dinners thrown that week to make sure that Bruce and JoJo would remember their friends in Umbria. But since they weren't actually leaving until after my birthday bash the following Saturday, the two celebrations collided head-on midweek at a big dinner party on the back patio of the Palazzaccio. My out-of-town guests had arrived—Ed and Barb; Barbara Bosson and her friend Sara from L.A.; Loring and Margarita from San Francisco (who had rented Bruce and JoJo's house for a year, giving them the means to go to Mexico); and David and Susan Liederman, who were already in the process of ravaging the countryside for small animals to roast in our *forno*. The farewell party celebrants joined up with the birthday party crowd and they all melded together into one pulsating party organism.

"More lambs! More pigs!" called out Liederman.

"And pizza. When we run out of local protein we'll cook pizzas for the rest of the night."

When David heard how celebrated Bruce's pizza was, he got competitively engaged. He wanted to go one-on-one with Bruce—dueling doughs. Bruce just smiled and told him that he abdicated the crown. He was already thinking about tortillas.

We told jokes that night—after dinner, when the Palazzaccio's giant house-bottle of grappa came to the table and was ceremoniously passed around and around. We told the old ones, the great ones. Half the people—the Italian/expat contingent—had never heard them before, and many of the rest of us had forgotten that we knew them, so it was like the first time. I don't recall ever laughing so much. The jokes are equal opportunity offenders—Jews, African-Americans, Japanese, Italians (especially the carabinieri) were all equally and properly disrespected. The two party crowds were now joined at the hip.

On Thursday, I brought a ringer in—just in case. I walked up the hill to speak to Benedetto, owner and impresario of Da Beppino. Could he provide some of his famous antipasto for the party? And some tables and chairs? And tablecloths and napkins?

"*Si, certo, con piacere.*" Yes, of course, with pleasure.

We decided on the antipasto—deer carpaccio, goose carpaccio, sausages in crust, roasted vegetables, *prosciutto in pane,* grilled tomatoes, melon and prosciutto and plates of assorted house-made *salume* and cheeses. All this would be on the tables when the guests arrived.

Jokes at the Palazzaccio

David decided we needed some kind of roasting pan with a grill for the pig, so we all went shopping. None of the kitchen stores had anything big enough, so we called Mayes and she directed us to a store that might have something. Under the highway in a very unscenic part of Trevi we found Raspa, a store unlike any other I've ever seen. They sell hardware, goldfish, lawn furniture, livestock feed and some very nice corduroy pants—everything except the out-sized grill pan that David needed. But he spied a rectangle of sheet metal propped up in the corner, asked the proprietor if he could borrow a sledgehammer and went to work banging this thing into the shape he needed. Then he rummaged through a pile of junk in the corner and came up with two pieces of open aluminum shelving that would fit side by side on top as a grill. We were all set.

On Friday, the day before our party, Liederman and I went on a tour of the butchers. First, of course, I took him to Ugo. We didn't order the pig from him because, being a purist, Ugo didn't feel this was the right time of year for a suckling pig. Yes, they could be found, but suckling pig—*maialino*—was a winter dish, for New Year's Eve. We did, however, taste some of his prosciutto and take the tour of the back of his shop where it's all made.

Then we went to Fabio, Lauro's son and heir. That's where we picked up the pig and the lamb. We also bought two chickens, because David wanted to test the oven. We would fire it up that night to make sure he understood its subtleties in preparation for the party the next day. We hauled the wrapped carcasses out to my VW Golf, looking like Mafia hit men after a long day at the office. On the way home, we stopped at Fortunati, my neighborhood truffle purveyor, where David picked out a few beautiful specimens to slice—razor-thin—and put under the skin of the chickens before roasting.

Barb, my sister-in-law, volunteered to be David's sous-chef—or slave—and learned more in the next twenty-four hours about the insides of chickens, pigs and lambs than she'd perhaps had in mind. She was stalwart, but I won't tell you the places her hand found itself. Ed and David and I built a pyre in the *forno* and fired it up. David marveled at the fact that the flue of the oven is on the outside, just above the opening; the oven chamber itself is a sealed vault so the fire vents out the door and straight up into the chimney—right in front of your face if you're putting something in the oven. This must have been a very effective form of population control back in the 1600s.

"This is a big fucking oven," said David solemnly, once

the roaring fire had turned the bricks white. "We're gonna have to wait a couple hours before we can put these chickens in. Ideally we should be doing pizzas now. This is a seriously hot oven."

Two hours later we roasted the truffled chickens. David said the oven was still too hot, but we were all hungry. By gingerly moving them in and out, David managed to cook them perfectly. He was getting into the oven now.

"We're going to roast the pig tonight. All night. By the time people arrive for the party tomorrow it'll be perfect. This is an incredible oven."

Much later, after we had eaten the chickens and cleaned up, we were all sitting outside under the pergola, chatting away. At about midnight, David said it was time. Barb, who had been second-in-command with rubbing, marinating, stuffing and buffing the *maialino,* helped David bring it out from the kitchen. And just before we all went off to bed, we loaded it into David's makeshift roasting pan and placed it in the coolest corner of the oven, away from the banked coals. We propped up the steel door over the mouth of the oven and all went off to sleep.

The next morning I woke up to the sound of tables and chairs being set up around the pool. Benedetto and two strong young men were setting up. I went down and offered him coffee. He checked out the construction of the *amplificazione* and was very pleased to see it was done properly—in the old style.

"*Buon lavoro,*" he muttered as he inspected the stonework. Given that we were his only neighbor within sight, he wanted to make sure that we hadn't trashed the neighborhood. Then he told his two helpers to pick me up and throw me into the pool. It was an Italian birthday tradition, apparently. I, not being a traditionalist, tried to resist, and Benedetto got a good laugh out of it.

"Tucker, tell him to take a look at this!" shouted David from the oven. He was taking his first look at the *maialino* that had been roasting all night.

Benedetto went to look as I dried off and followed. The pig was a dark, almost purplish color. At first I thought it was overdone.

"No. *É perfetto*," proclaimed Benedetto, who specialized in such things. He tapped the hard skin to test its crispness. He looked at David with a look of obvious respect. David stood proudly next to the pig, like a hunter who had just bagged his first rhino.

"We'll just leave it until later. Cover it up so the bugs don't get it. Room temperature will be perfect."

Benedetto asked what time the guests were arriving and

Kids in the pool

then told me everything would be set up and waiting for them. He asked if I needed wine, but I told him we had taken care of it. Susan had scoured the Montefalco area and come back with more wine than we thought we could possibly drink. We were wrong, of course.

At one o'clock sharp, George arrived with Mariane and two cases of perfectly chilled Prosecco. All forty or so of the other guests showed up within fifteen minutes of them. Unlike in America, where people are often fashionably late, this crowd arrived hungry and ready to dive in.

Although we had tables and chairs set up around the pool and down toward the *bocce* court, everyone congregated under the pergola. It's a powerful magnet, it seems. People pulled up chairs two deep around the table and then others just stood behind them. The food and drink were set up buffet style on tables next to the *forno* and everyone just helped themselves. The antipasti from Da Beppino—which was enough food to feed the Italian Army on maneuvers—was being inhaled at startling speed. The *salsicce in crosto,* which are the Umbrian version of pigs in a blanket, were gone within fifteen minutes. We made a space in the middle of the table and Liederman uncovered the pig and brought it in, to a round of applause. This, too, was sliced into, savored (there is nothing—nothing—that's better-tasting than Umbrian pork) and gone within the hour. It was a frenzy; it was like locusts.

"Mikey, I'm gonna change up the agenda," said David, in a little bit of a panic. "I'm gonna crank up the oven and do the pizza first—while the oven is hot. We'll save the lamb for this evening. This crowd can eat."

Some people had brought bathing suits to take advantage of the pool; those who forgot just swam in their underwear. The *bocce* court was fully engaged. And the afternoon passed into evening in a blink. The oven, which is only steps away from the pergola, was a magnet as well. The whole party eventually gathered in this area—the chairs around the table now three-deep, the finished pizzas landing rhythmically every three minutes or so, to great whoops and shouts. The lamb, trussed and ready, waited its turn for glory.

When the sun dropped low in the sky and the pizzas slowed down, Jill tapped a spoon against her wineglass to get everyone's attention so she could give me my birthday present; a beautiful rendition of "I Can't Give You Anything but Love." She started with the verse that goes:

> "Now that it's your birthday, I don't know what to do;
> Can't give you a Thunderbird or a penthouse with a
>   view;
> Can't even buy a little gift;
> I'm much too broke, I find.
> But there is one way to save the day;
> And I sure hope you don't mind
> That . . .
> I Can't Give You Anything but Love, Baby. . . ."

She sang it slow and sexy, with innuendo fairly dripping, and with one elegant gesture to the house construction and the pool she made it crystal clear why we could no longer afford anything but love.

I sat there, feeling quite like a pasha, with all these happy, sated folks around me—my brother, who's become a good friend after all these years, this gathering of new acquaintances and old standbys. And what came to mind were all the people who weren't there. The thing about Jill and my leaping off the edge together is that we tend to leave

The remains of the pig

people behind. We don't leave them on purpose; nor do we leave them forever—we often reconnect at another place and time. But right at the moment of departure, I can see how it might feel like we had taken the party away. Some dear friends in L.A. were upset when we unceremoniously left for Marin. Now, people in Marin were feeling much the same way. Caroline, whose issues of abandonment go back much further than her relationship with us, felt particularly lost when we abruptly sold our house and moved to New York, taking with us a lifestyle and an energy that she had grown to count on.

Across the table were Bruce and JoJo, looking as happy and relaxed as I've ever seen them. In two days, they'd be off to Mexico for a year at least, flying without a net, living on a shoestring, leaving us all behind to somehow manage without them. They didn't seem to be carrying any guilt about it at all.

"Fuck it," their shining faces seemed to say. "Get over it."

Fuck it, indeed. To have the partner of a lifetime—for a lifetime—is rare stuff. We'd be fools not to indulge it to the limit. What extraordinary freedom it is not to care about up or down, rich or poor, East Coast, West Coast, as long as we're in the taxi together. "Up and down are just directions," said one of our gurus in Marin, "and there's a hell of a lot of fun to be had either way."

"Lamb's ready!" shouted Liederman from the *forno,* and we all scurried to make room in the center of the table.

Acknowledgments

Thanks to my agents, Jane Dystel and Miriam Goderich, for encouraging me to write this book. And to my editors, Eric Price and Morgan Entrekin, for encouraging me to write it better. Much appreciation is due to all my Italian teachers, especially Wendy Walsh in Mill Valley, who also came up with the wonderful quote from Verdi. A blanket apology is due all my friends in Umbria whose lives I exposed, and to Umbria itself whose bountiful pleasures are secrets no more.